LESSONS FROM A BALD

CHICK

Mary Beth Hall

BookLocker.com, Inc.
2009

Dedication

To my King.

To Mom, who dances with our King.

The author believes in leaving this world a better place than when she arrived. The proceeds from this book are intended as donations to individuals battling cancer. It is her hope and desire as these individuals are blessed, they, in turn, give to someone else in need, thus changing our world one small corner at a time. We change the world when we take the focus off ourselves.

"And whatever you do in word or deed, do all in the name of the Lord Jesus, giving thanks to God the Father through Him".

Colossians 3:17

Table of Contents

Normalcy is Overrated

I am a 46-year-old wife, mom, guidance counselor, and Christian; not necessarily in that order. So far, I have been in education 22 years as an elementary teacher, middle school teacher, writing teacher, special education teacher, reading specialist, university instructor, and counselor. I have an undergraduate degree in special education and regular education, a master's degree in administration, a master's degree in counseling, and certification for school principal. All of these degrees mean one thing only; I am flat broke.

I am not normal.

When my kids burp at the dinner table I rate them on a scale of one to ten and loudly chastise them if they score anything below five. I've threatened them on occasion for anything below a three. I try to keep other bodily noises to a minimum (at least at the dinner table), so I think I get points for that. I've taught my sons since they were old enough to kick a ball that it doesn't matter if you win or lose, what matters is how your hair looks while you are playing. I tell them every winter in all sincerity not to eat yellow snow. I am convinced when their friends come over they come to play with me and seeing my boys is just an added benefit. I like to serve meals as if I am the waitress and when I put the plate in front of each person I love to say with life or death severity, "Now, this plate is very hot. Be veeeerrrrrry careful". Sometimes I serve meals of only one color. I love pajama parties. I believe pumpkin pie is a breakfast food. Tipping the whipped cream canister completely upside down and squirting as much as possible into each other's mouths and dousing the floor, cabinets, refrigerator, and sometimes ceiling is huge fun in my world. My boys get in big trouble when their father walks in the kitchen and sees the mess. They innocently point their fingers at me because yes, I started it. I am not right. I admit that.

I am married to a prince. When he reprimands the boys for slurping loudly from their cereal bowls and they protest I taught them cereal tastes better this way, he doesn't chastise me (in front of them). When the boys and I have pajama parties and the son in the top bunk sits up in his sleep and gets whacked in the head by the ceiling fan, resulting in a blood bath and an emergency room visit at 4:00 a.m. and double-digit stitches, my prince just shakes his head, mumbles to himself about not understanding why we can't sleep in our own beds like normal people, and starts spending excessive amounts of time by himself in the garage sitting in his boat. At these times I try scaling back on my behaviors to get him out of his boat, but so far I'm not having much luck. I saw him moving his shaving gear and pillow in there the other day.

My husband treats me like a queen. On the next April Fool's Day we will be married 20 years. I am acutely aware I do not deserve this man. He is a gift straight from the hands of God. Why God was mad at him and sacked him with me I will never know. All I can do is keep thanking God for him and pray this man never learns what I am really like.

Curtis and I are complete opposites but we are both in love with the same person; me. Oh yeah, and God. We started our marriage on our wedding night praying together in our hotel room. I told him once if either of us ever stopped reading our Bibles we were doomed. He responded with a look that summed it up in one word: "Duh!" Our focus on God is what keeps us on track and steady through the years. This involves knowing God through having a relationship with Him. I've known God since I was 25 years old, and I have learned He is a God who keeps His promises. I've learned He has many facets to His personality, and I plan to spend the rest of my life learning about them. One of my favorites is His great sense of humor.

I met my husband by teaching next door to him. I thought Curtis was the nicest guy I had ever met. As we got to know one another and share about our daily lives it became apparent I did not approve of the girls he dated. In my opinion, these ditzy girls didn't deserve such a man of deep quality. Although he didn't ask for it, I told Curtis my opinion often. I'm surprised the guy ever spoke to me at all during that school year.

Since I had such strong opinions about this nice guy, I began praying for him. In my deluded mind I believed a nice and kind man deserved a sweet and gentle woman. I asked God to send Curtis the sweetest, most gentle, quiet, and meek woman He ever created. I kept telling God Curtis deserved this type of person in his life. I begged God on Curtis' behalf during my morning commutes to work. I specifically asked for this woman to be madly in love with Curtis and treat him the special way he deserved. This went on for many months.

When Curtis and I dated and later married, I laughed at what God had done. Yes, He gave Curtis a woman who loved him, but sweet, kind, meek, and gentle have never been adjectives attached to me. Curtis got a mouthy, opinionated, strong-willed, determined, immature, impulsive bride. Poor guy! All those mornings praying for Curtis's wife probably had God laughing because He knew who He had in mind for Curtis, and it sure wasn't the Southern belle I was asking for. Yes, God has a sense of humor. A bit warped, in my opinion, but still a good one.

Our courtship lasted one year. I became a Christian three years before I met Curtis and after spending seven years in a relationship that was a big fat waste of time I asked God to pick out my husband for me. I gave God my standard list of qualifications and asked Him to get back to me when He was ready to fill my prescription. I asked Him if it wasn't too big of an inconvenience could he sort of hurry up because I didn't feel like waiting long. I completely trusted God to take care of this for me.

Curtis and I started dating completely without my knowledge. We had a spaghetti dinner fundraiser at school and Curtis and I were delegated to purchase the paper products one Saturday. He picked me up at my apartment and we went shopping and then to lunch. I didn't know until much later that Curtis considered that our first date. I don't know what he considered the date I had with someone else later that night.

I have spent the last 19 years realizing anew what a gift from God this man is. God not only filled my order completely, but He went above and beyond what I had asked for and gave me a man with qualities that I didn't even know I needed or wanted in a mate. That is so like God; to not only fill the cup, but make it run over. I am so glad I had the good sense to ask God to pick out my husband and then even better sense to wait until He did.

Stubborn Ox

This husband I got from God is a frustrating, irritating, and stubborn ox. When the yearly form letter came reminding me to have my mammogram Curtis immediately demanded to know when I was going to have it done. I told him I would call for the appointment soon. He proceeded to harass, annoy, and badger me until I knew the only way to shut the guy up was to make the appointment.

Like a good girl I had my yearly mammogram on spring break. As an educator, I usually have my mammograms during the summer when I have more leisure time and my days are full of huge decisions such as which side to turn onto while on the hammock, but I was mad at God last summer because I was not getting the job I wanted. Being the spiritually mature person that I am I was too busy trying to force God's hand (a COMPLETE waste of time, do not try it) that I put off my mammogram until I had another stretch of free time, which was spring break.

Before spring break I noticed I was unusually tired and not rested after naps. I have a black belt in napping, so for my naps to backfire on me and leave me drained caused me to think two things. One, that I was pregnant, which would result in big fat YIPPEES from me and a not so big fat yippee from Curtis who informed me years before when I thought I wanted to have another baby that

I was too old. This resulted in my extremely quick-witted (so quick it was almost genius. Sometimes I amaze myself) comment that my boyfriend didn't think so. Hilarious, if you ask me. Immature, if you ask Curtis.

The other scenario I envisioned for my fatigue was that I was dying from a terrible disease. This is exactly what I told Curtis and others who were getting suspicious and asking questions about my lethargy. My co-worker started getting suspicious one day when I was at my computer for an awfully long time without typing or clicking the mouse. My back was to her and she thought I was reading an extremely long message. It turned out I was sound asleep in the middle of the day sitting upright at my computer. I think I started getting suspicious then, too. Usually when I sleep at work I curl up under my desk where nobody can find me. Sleeping out in the open like that was crossing even my boundary lines and was, well, embarrassing.

Anyway, those were my two scenarios. I was hoping for the former because I adore every single thing about babies and motherhood (except potty training, which really should have been taken care of by God before He sent me the smelly little angels) and the latter, which although I was saying I was dying from a terrible disease I didn't really believe it. That happened to other people. This left me with just being tired.

So, I was tired. I would get over it. It was my blood thinning out for the upcoming summer. In winter I always used the excuse for a nap on the completely scientific fact made up by me that my blood was thickening for the cold months ahead. Never mind that during this time every show I watched seemed to have a cancer victim, every book I picked up had a cancer topic, and every conversation somehow included cancer. I could not get away from cancer. I started having that "Uh Oh Feeling" inside that God was trying to get my attention on something that I was not interested in having my attention gotten on, so like the mature and deeply spiritual person that I am, I ignored it all as best I could.

When the woman who performed my mammogram, whom I like to secretly call the Very-Evil-Person-Who-Squashed-Me-Flatter-Than-God-Never-Intended (okay, maybe I don't secretly call her that, maybe I actually screamed that at her while cradling my limp flattened self) came back in the mammogram room and said in her very evil voice,

"Ha ha ha, now we've got you, don't think you can run from us, Sucker!"

Or maybe she said,

"We need to take a few more pictures, you weren't quite on there all the way," the "Uh Oh Feeling" returned in full force, accompanied by its good friend, the "Oh No Feeling". I told myself to stop being silly. Tons of women have to stay and have more fun having another mammogram. It happens all the time. It means absolutely nothing. The fact that God kept reminding me He was there and would never leave me meant nothing.....really. I happily went home to reinflate myself and play very hard on spring break, which consisted of painting a different room every day in our house (I know, I'm a party animal) and ignore the fact that I am a horrible painter and create bigger messes that take more time to clean up than to actually paint the entire room.

LESSON: Denial works………… sort of.

Thursdays Cannot Be Trusted

My mammogram was on Thursday. I painted my son's bedroom the following Monday. I'm a really quick painter so it took me only nine hours. I took a lunch break and watched ten minutes of television during which the movie I landed on had a breast cancer victim and the two commercials I saw in my haste to change the channel were about cancer medications. Enough TV, time to get back to destroying my son's room.

Sweetie came home from work, (he is a big important superintendant of a school system) and promptly declared that I made the usual big fat mess of the room, and why didn't I at least take off the light switch covers instead of trying to paint around them? I followed him around the house, pouting, sighing loudly, and dragging my knuckles on the ground in defeat until he finally assured me that the room was fine and he was glad he does not go in there often. My feelings pacified, I then went about welcoming home from school my two reasons for existing; Alex, age 15 and Benjamin, age 13, and then happily proceeded to burn dinner.

The next day I could not hold my head up and spent the day on the couch reading. I was worn out from all of that painting and really, thinking I would paint a whole room a day was probably biting off more than I could chew and I should change my goal to painting a room, which I already did, which meant I could spend the rest of the week on the couch reading because my blood was still scientifically thinning, which is precisely what I did.

The phone rang and I saw on caller ID it was the hospital. I somehow knew before they even said it that I was being cordially invited back for more fun and games with the mammogram machine. This time they were going to add an ultrasound to the party and to come in three days. When the phone rang again and it was my doctor's office making sure I got the call from the hospital, I assured myself this was efficient medicine at its best and thanked them for calling.

When the phone rang a third time and it was the mammogram center making sure I got the call to come back I started thinking of filing harassment charges. What was the big deal? Tons of women get called back daily, the lady on the phone said so and even added that statistically eight out of ten call backs (where am I Hollywood? Not as much fun as I envisioned) were perfectly fine. So there! I was going to be the eight out of ten. God whispering to me, "I will never leave you nor forsake you" was just His way of saying hi.

Being the good girl that I am, plus my stubborn husband threatening me, I went back to the very nice and homey and warm and comforting mammogram center at the hospital. I was actually on time to show everyone that I was not frightened; I was eight out of ten. I even entertained the idea of doing a bit of shopping afterward since I was a woman of leisure on spring break. It didn't matter that I entertain the idea of shopping on a daily basis. The crucial part was I knew I would have the appropriate mind set and attitude for shopping after the mammogram party.

It turned out I did not have the appropriate mind set for shopping. I had the mind set of needing someone to get me off the cliff I was mentally hurtling myself off of. I realized too late that I needed Husband, whom I ignorantly previously assured did not need to go with me.

The important medical people performed the mammogram and the ultrasound, and the nice doctor lady came in and told me they found something that needed a biopsy (YIKES!) and blah, blah, blah...... I heard nothing the nice doctor lady was saying after that.

Lesson: Do not go to your second mammogram alone, ever.

I suppose this is the time to share my mom died of breast cancer at the age of 67 when I was too young to be without a mother, which, in my opinion is any age. I happened to be 36 years old at the time. I remembered her biopsy experience as very traumatic for her, and so I immediately retreated to my Happy Place in my mind which consisted of considering what to burn for dinner and wondering what time my Darlings would be home from school.

I then thanked everyone for the lovely party and insisted I really must go and proceeded to drive to my husband's school where I hoped he could put it all into perfect perspective for me, or at the bare minimum take over some of the hysteria for me. Somewhere amidst all of the fun they gave me an appointment card with the biopsy date.

This time I invited Hubby to the festivities. The nurses, doctors, and radiologist who performed the procedure were calm and orderly. I was an emotional wreck. I knew. I knew the radiologist knew. I was sure the doctor knew. The only thing the nurse knew was if they didn't hurry up and finish she would qualify for disability because I was crushing her hand. When it was over I crashed blindly through the hallways crying and blubbering and heaving myself at Hubby who I hoped would get me the heck out of there. As I threw myself out the main door I heard the receptionist call out, "Have a nice day!" Absolutely nothing made sense in this world anymore.

My sweetie and I sat in the car until I was finished secreting nasal mucous all over his suit and tie and then he promptly did the one thing on earth that makes everything better. He offered to take me out for breakfast.

LESSON: Do not go to these things alone. Someone is sure to buy you a meal.

When in Doubt, Party

I died a thousand deaths between the time of the mammogram, the ultrasound, the biopsy, and the ultimate diagnosis. I spent a lot of time seriously thinking which outfit would make me look the thinnest in my coffin. Finally, the day came that would reveal the test results. I wore my favorite outfit to hear the results because I thought if I'm going to have cancer (which I talked myself into NOT having), I was going to impress everyone with how cute I was. The radiologist who performed my biopsy came in and completely and rudely ignoring my cute outfit said he was very sorry to tell me that I had breast cancer. Upon hearing the results, being the deeply spiritual person that I am, of course my first thoughts went directly to God and they went just like this,

"Ohgod,ohgod,ohgod,ohgod,ohgod,ohgod,ohgod, ohgod,ohgod,ohgod,ohgod,ohgod!"

The radiologist had a lot to say and it went like this,

"Cancer…blah…blah…surgery…treatments……. ohgododohgod…..stage……blahblahblahblah…ohgod…. sugery…….oncologist…lymph nodes….ohgod……"

I'm pretty sure the ohgod's were mine, but I couldn't say my name at that point so I'll just guess. At this time I decided to show my intelligence and my ability to think under pressure, and so I asked a series of questions that went like this, "lkjhguwrg? Tuajklvbgj? Jrkahtuatuyt845y? 78halkhjhgjhg? Fjhfhgtuxur?"

At this point I let my husband take over. I retreated deep into myself and thought,

"My babies, my babies, my babies, please God, no........."

I mentally curled into a fetal position thinking no mother should ever have to agonize over her children this way. Surely God wouldn't tear us apart from one another, would He?

We somehow made it out of there alive with another appointment card crushed in my palm to meet with the surgeon the next week. We got in the car and being the deeply spiritual and mature person that I already said I am, I began to lie. The first lie went like this,

"I can do breast cancer, Honey. I've never done breast cancer, this will be something new. I can do this. Really. It will be fine."

Then we called our good friends who were packed and ready to visit their daughter in Italy but were waiting by the phone for us to call before leaving for the airport. I then proceeded with my next lie and it went like this,

"Hi Debbie. Yes, everything is fine. Have a great trip, I'll be thinking about you. What was it on the mammogram? Oh, the doctor said it was some flukey-type thingamajingy that just showed up but now is gone.

Weird, huh? What took so long? Oh, they couldn't find the radiologist who performed the biopsy and we had to wait for him because they like to have the person who did the procedure give the results, and......What? Put Curtis on the phone? Okay, here he is".

My Sweetie then promptly TOLD THE TRUTH! What was he thinking? They were leaving for Italy for two weeks for crying out loud (which I was at this point). Telling the truth would ruin their entire trip. Hello! Am I the only one getting this?

Sweetie, crying, handed the phone back to me with the admonition that I should not lie to my friends. Who was he to admonish me? I have cancer here! Before I could even begin to think how I could throw this diagnosis around to start getting my own way from now on I heard the words that were a balm to my tortured emotions,

"MB, we are going to get you through this. Do you hear me? We are going to get you through this. I promise, we will."

Sigh....... Finally some words I actually wanted to hear. I could then go home and lie to my family.

LESSON: Wearing cute clothes does not help the diagnosis, but try it anyway.

We drove to my Sweetie's parents' house. They are the most wonderful people God ever created. I love

them so much that I once shared with them my deepest
feelings for them and said if anything ever happened to
them I absolutely would never recover. They were so
touched by my statement that they laughed (in my face!)
and told me that they couldn't be here forever. They may
have also added that it would be wise for me to grow up,
but I'm not sure. Anyway, we drove to their house and
ruined their lives with the news. They were completely
devastated (they sort of like me, too). After ruining their
day, we decided to go home. We decided not to tell our
boys until we knew exactly what we were dealing with. A
slow and agonizing death was what we were dealing with
as far as I was concerned. I tend to think on the positive
side of things.

I have five sisters and two brothers. I am number
seven out of eight kids. I called sister number five from
the car. No answer. I called sister number two and
couldn't reach her. I called sister number three. No luck.
Suddenly, everyone had a fantastic life without cancer
and they were all busy living it. I called number two's
husband. He called number two. She called me, and I
ruined her day. She called the others and ruined their
days. By the time we got home the phone was ringing
nonstop. One call was asking if my husband wanted to be
a server at the Ladies' Banquet at church. Another wanted
to know if we would be so kind as to donate money to a
local university. Really, there were lots of calls in there
about me, too. We realized we could not keep the news
from the boys and were concerned they would hear it

from someone else, like maybe a telemarketer, so we decided to tell them. We called them to the family room.

I have wonderful boys. They are smart, witty, and huge. One is 6'2" and the other 5'10" but in my opinion they still fit perfectly on my lap. As a family, we meet on these couches in the family room in the evenings and have family devotions and prayer time, so they weren't curious as to why we were there. Granted, we never had our devotions before dinner, but they were completely unsuspecting. The four of us sat on the couches in the family room and I began:

"Do you know what cancer is?"

DUH!

They said yes, they knew what cancer was. I think I saw them roll their eyes, but I decided to let that pass. I then proceeded to very delicately sugarcoat the entire situation by telling them that we were just at the doctor's office and that I had a "spot" of something that they were calling cancer. I told them it was no big deal, the doctors were going to get it out, I was not scared, they did not need to be scared, I was not scared, do not be scared, I was not scared, no big deal. I did coat it in some truth by telling them God was not surprised, He would be taking care of me, this was a great opportunity to show others what a relationship with God is like, and I was thanking God for this because He says; "Give thanks in all things".

Curtis added some mature statements and then led us in prayer. During the prayer he thanked God for my breast cancer and told God he knew He was in control of the situation. After we prayed I went into the kitchen to see what I could burn for dinner. It turned out to be ribs.

The phone and doorbell were still ringing.

Friends showed up bearing gifts, and I did what I naturally do whenever three or more are gathered in my name. I had a party. A billiards party. Curtis had very recently finished building a new room in the basement for a pool table and this was the perfect opportunity to christen it with a party. We called my in-laws and invited them to a pool tournament in our new billiards room. They came immediately. The boys love a party (they are my sons, after all) and amongst the telephone and doorbell ringing, friends showing up, and utter chaos, we partied.

Being the excellent counselor that I try to tell myself I am, I waited some time for my sons to process the bomb we dropped on them and then I sought them out individually. I caught my 13 year old in the kitchen and asked him what he thought about our news. He cautiously shared that he was worried and confused. He said as long as they got the cancer out then he would be okay. I assured him they would get it out. He shared that he agreed it was a great opportunity to show others what a relationship with God is all about. He ended by agreeing it could even be a good thing. I added my standard lie that I was not scared.

Later, I sought out my 15 year old. I found him in the kitchen, also. (No surprise that is where I'd find both teen-age boys.) I asked him what he was thinking. His exact response,

"I don't like it. I don't like it a lot".

I reminded him that God was in complete control and I was not scared. (It's okay to lie if you put a truth with it, right?) I assured him it was going to be fine and they would get the cancer out in surgery (I hoped). I reminded him that God was not surprised and that Curtis and I were thanking God for it. Emotional check on my boys accomplished, I rejoined the party downstairs.

LESSON: Use every situation as an excuse to party.

Our poor friends who were on their way to Italy were shell shocked by my diagnosis. They called me from their car. They called me from the airport. They called me from the airplane. Gailen is Debbie's husband. He and I have one love in common; food. He did what any good friend would do in the midst of a crisis. He asked me to help him decide what to have from the airplane menu. I think I told him to go with the pork chops. Menu accomplished, he told me he and Debbie would help get me though this, God was in control, and I would be living my beliefs out loud. He then continued to encourage me by telling me not to "blow it".

My brothers and sisters were instructed not to call yet because we weren't telling the boys. They didn't know we went ahead and told them, and throughout the shock and chaos of that first evening I didn't realize they were at their own homes devastated and in shock and unable to reach me.

My family general doctor is also my neighbor. She is an excellent doctor. She came into my house that evening terribly upset. She was crying and hugging me. I was trying to create a calm and peaceful atmosphere in the house and her emotional display was not matching my precariously balanced and constructed mood of the house. My anxiety level was rising for fear the boys would come in and witness this and catch on that the issue was bigger than the one I had sugarcoated.

She wanted to quit being a doctor because she gets too upset when things like this happen to her good patients. I was a good patient? Not for long...... She then talked about other reasons why she didn't like her job. Being the good counselor that I am, I maintained eye contact with her while I gave her a free counseling session in my kitchen amongst the voices in my head screaming,

"I HAVE CANCER! OH GOD! PLEASE HELP ME!"

After experiencing many times when telling someone my news and the person immediately telling me all of their problems in great detail, turning me into the counselor again and again, I wondered what was happening. Counseling is a tiring profession. A counselor doesn't just listen. A counselor actively listens. This is a verb. It means staying involved, maintaining eye contact, responding, and "being there". Why were people putting me in this position when I was already tired from the cancer and the shock? It was completely wearing me out.

I've since come to the mature realization that we judge others by their actions and judge ourselves by our motives. I needed to focus on others' intended motives, regardless of their actions or words. Sometimes I amaze myself with my maturity. I've decided when I grow up I want to be just like me.

LESSON: When someone tells you devastating news, do not turn the conversation back to yourself. Focus on that person. Make no "I" or "me" statements throughout the entire conversation. This is not about you (unless the statement is something like this, "I would like for you to let me give you one million dollars". Then you can use "I" and "me" all you want). Unfortunately the "I" and "me" statements I got did not involve any of this.

A doctor friend from church called. We talked at length about procedures, techniques, and advancements in medicine, and then he said something wonderful. He shared when he heard the news at the hospital about my diagnosis he got excited because he sees God allowing these things to happen to people who will glorify Him throughout it. What a beautiful statement for my raw emotions. I hoped I was up to that task.

I stopped myself from verbalizing that I really and truly hoped God would never be so kind as to allow him the same honor one day. I simply ooze maturity.

LESSON: Say something beautiful.

Maturity Doesn't Work

Instead of staying home in shock the next day, I acted like a mature and responsible adult and went to work. I was standing in the hallway among hundreds of rushing, talking, hitting, flirting, laughing (the nerve!) adolescents when a teacher friend came to me and asked THE QUESTION. I responded,

"The good news is my hair looks really cute today. The bad news is I have breast cancer".

He then did the perfect thing. He told me he loved me and all of the reasons why (it took three seconds). I soaked up every word. I had only known him for six months, but I considered that plenty of time to get to know me enough to love me.

LESSON: Remind the person with a diagnosis why he or she is important to you.

Another teacher friend asked me THE QUESTION. When I told her she then proceeded to tell me all about her health and marriage problems, thus making me the counselor for a 45 minute session. I was exhausted.

LESSON: See above lesson about who you are to focus on. See above as a reminder about focusing on motives, too.

I went to church the following Sunday. The very first person I told said;

"Gee, are you scared? I know a lot of people who died from that. You know so-and-so's sister? Her mom died from breast cancer. And do you know such-n-such's third removed cousin? She died a horrible death from it, too, and then there's ...."

I missed the rest of the conversation because I was busy shoving people down, clawing their backs, and stomping on their bodies to get out of there.

LESSON: Refrain from saying stupid things to the person with a diagnosis. If you cannot refrain from saying stupid things, do not talk at all. Just shut up. (If someone says something like the above to you, you do not have to focus on their motive. You have my permission to determine the person is an idiot and say bad things about him over and over in your mind).

Amidst this time of telling people "the news" I decided I should clarify things with my sons. I told them,

"Yes, I have a spot on my breast and yes, it has cancer, but others are going to want to call it breast cancer, and that's okay with me if that is what they want to call it so let's get used to the idea of hearing those words by saying them out loud".

We then had fun practicing saying the words "breast cancer" until I was convinced they could hear it

LESSONS FROM A BALD CHICK

without flinching. I don't know what I was thinking because I still couldn't hear the words without flinching.

I hoped I was not causing my teen-aged sons to fixate on breasts because I knew my boys would never fixate on breasts on their own. Denial is a beautiful thing.

Dress Rehearsal

It was April and I was in our church Easter play. I secretly wanted to be Jesus, but year after year I was passed over for the part. I thought I would make an excellent Jesus, but nobody was asking me. I think it was the whole breast issue, you know, hanging on that cross with hardly nothing on. I should have known then these breasts were going to be nothing but trouble.

It was Thursday night dress rehearsal. My biopsy was the next morning. We went through the performance once and were in the middle of a ten-minute break. I was emotionally shattered. The church lights were out. The cast, choir, and orchestra were sitting in pews chatting, practicing their lines and songs and notes, or joking around. Normally, I would be right there with the people goofing off. Instead, I wanted to be by myself. I sat alone in the dark. I couldn't hold it together another minute. I hung my head and cried out to God,

"Lord, I am so alone here. I am so scared. I cannot do this biopsy tomorrow. I need someone to talk to. Please send someone to talk with me. Please, Lord, I desperately need someone. I am in the midst of all these Christians and I am so alone. Please help me. I am begging you! I need your help. I am so alone....."

At that time a friend from my Sunday School class came over and said she had my calendar because we have the same purses and I accidentally put mine in her purse at rehearsal the night before. (I hoped I didn't accidentally take out lunch money for tomorrow, too). She asked if I wanted her to go get it. I nodded. When she came back she sat in the pew in front of me and turned around to face me. She put her hand on my knee, looked me in the eyes, and said,

"So, MB, How are you?"

I burst into tears, scaring her to death.

I told her all that I was going through. I told her I had just finished begging God to send someone over to ask me exactly what she asked. I shared my fears relating to the biopsy in the morning, the strain of the past weeks of worry, the fear of the unknown, the certainty that I was going to die, and the horribleness that was currently my life. She listened intently. She heard what I was saying and what I was not saying. Then she prayed for me. And then she missed her cue to be up on stage to start the second rehearsal. Since it was dress rehearsal night we operate under the rule "the show must go on" regardless of any mishaps. To put it mildly, our director was not impressed or encouraged when the opening narrator was not in her spot narrating when the lights went up.

I, on the other hand, was greatly encouraged. God heard my cry for help and sent someone to talk and pray with me. I knew then that He would get me through tomorrow's biopsy and anything after that. Of course I already knew that in my head, but my heart needed the reassurance. I was so very encouraged.

Until I went into the Lost and Found.

I was looking for something; an umbrella, a Bible one of the boys left behind, a book, a jacket, or some other item we all seem to lose in church. The shelves were stacked with items and in an awkward spot. I had to lean in through the half doorway and scrounge around in darkness because I couldn't find the light switch. My hand was landing on items and my brain was registering whether that was the item I was seeking or not before my hand would seek out another object. My hand landed on a thin plastic book-shaped item. I brought it out into the light. It was a DVD with the title "Living with Your Breast Cancer". I stared, horrified. My brain was in shock, my emotions were screaming,

"No.....Lord,....please.....no.....please,.......just please............You cannot ask this of me, ... No!"

I couldn't run away any longer from what the Lord was telling me. And so I talked to Him. I made up with Him for my foolish tantrums regarding my job. I asked for forgiveness for being a brat. I acknowledged He was rightfully on the throne, there was no other God in my life, and I would continually follow Him all the days of my life. I praised Him for who He was. I praised Him for sending a friend to talk to me that night. I praised Him for tomorrow's biopsy. I praised Him for the future biopsy results. I gave thanks in all things. God's peace flowed over me like a soft velvet cloak. I wrapped and snuggled myself in it and went back to rehearsal.

I was so much better when it was time for me to say my part on stage that night. Unlike the narrator, I didn't even miss my cue.

I rushed home to wake Curtis up and share what God did for me that night. He was in a deep sleep and thought we were being attacked by aliens who were trying to steal his boat and therefore didn't have a clue as to what I was saying, but I was still encouraged.

Lesson: Whatever it is, thank God for it. Really.

Friends Come In All Sizes. Forgive Them If They Are A Size 2.

My house looked like a funeral home. Word was out about me. I can only guess it's because people really like who I am married to that the doorbell was constantly ringing and flowers and fruit baskets were being delivered. It was astonishing. Do I even know this many people? Do I actually know people who would spend money on flowers, gorgeously arranged fruit, and decadent items dipped in chocolate for me? Did everyone have the right address?

Not caring if it was the right address or not, I arranged the flowers and ate the chocolate. My house smelled great, my life fell apart. I started missing school for doctor appointments and surgery. The surgery was scheduled to remove the cancerous tumor and a suspect spot near it (two spots?), remove one or more lymph nodes depending on cancer involvement (oh God), and implant a port-a-catheter to receive future chemotherapy treatments (please, no) before the radiation treatments (I can't breathe).

My surgery was on a Thursday. On the morning of the surgery I bravely went to the hospital. I wanted the cancer out so I did not even mind getting there early. Husband is a morning person; me, not so much. Including the mammogram, this was the second time in my life I was early for something. So this is how the rest of the world functions. Very interesting. I was ready to be without cancer. I was horrified about the possibilities regarding the lymph node involvement, staging of the cancer, and the following treatments.

I was prepped and ready. The surgeon was not. I waited; thirsty and hungry. Two people at a time were allowed to come back to the pre-op room to wait with me. My husband was not one of them.

My Prince Charming has a total medical phobia. He has a lifetime of dealing with tumors in his head and developed a fear of all things medical. He has had seven craniotomies, the first one occurring when he was 18 months old. The tumors grew as he grew and wreaked havoc on his optical nerves by twisting around them and causing the doctors to cut the nerves, thus causing him to lose his left eye. He had part of his skull cut out, his face taken off (they put it back on), and a myriad of other procedures to get the hemangiomas and lymphangiomas out.

Didn't work. He still has a head full of them.

He likes to have guests over and entertain them after dinner by pulling at his closed eyelid and showing them part of a tumor that has flattened itself under his cheek and grown toward his ear. Why our guests are never fascinated by this but always suddenly have an emergency at home they must attend to completely escapes him. He likes to call this "Tumor Time". I like to call it "How To Lose Your Friends And Be Alone Forever And Ever".

So, in my opinion, my adorable husband had rightfully earned this medical phobia and the right to be absent at my bedside before my surgery. He and I knew that one sight of the I.V. would cause him to slither to the floor like a drunken gorilla and cause havoc with the medical staff. Besides, he and I also knew this was all about me and having to deal with him fainting would cause the focus to be where it shouldn't be; off of me. Therefore, I was happy to hold court at my bedside with my sisters, in laws, friends, and medical staff. They kept me entertained, which is exactly what I needed.

Lesson: See above lesson for how to turn every situation into a party.

I came out of the surgery not being able to see a thing, hurting, and confused. They gave me my glasses, morphine, and told me where I was. Somehow my sisters, mother-in-law and husband appeared at my recovery room bedside. The nurse informed me when I could dress myself I could go home. So, in front of all those people I attempted to dress, thus exposing everyone to the sad shape of my underwear. A sister immediately went out and bought me three new packs of underwear with four undies in each pack. I told her I think of her every five days when I put on a fresh pair. (Kidding).

Somehow I got home and was fed and put to bed. Dinner had arrived while I was gone in the form of salad, lasagna, and dessert from two friends who are both maybe a size two if they are soaking wet with rocks in their pockets. I forgave them for their single digit sizes by eating their meal. I kissed my sons, mumbled something about "Danger Zone" while pointing to my breast area, and slept the rest of the night away. My mother-in-law spent the night to keep close watch over me. I believe in all things Pajama Party but I couldn't muster the party atmosphere this night and just slept. Maturity means knowing when to party and when to sleep.

Lesson: Take some time to assess all under garments before every new situation.

The next day I was up cleaning the house (they must have done something truly remarkable to my brain), receiving more flowers, fruit baskets, meals, and visitors. It was a great day to not be at work.

I spent the weekend much the same.

I was cancer free (I hoped).

I went back to work the following Monday.

It was bit early to be back at work. I realized this when I couldn't keep my head up by 10:00 a.m. and went out to my car on my break and slept and nobody could find me. I think I deserve major points for being back at work though.

I believed I needed to be at school because our state testing began on that day and would continue for two weeks. Our education system is completely out of control. We base everything on The Tests. Careers are made or ruined by The Tests. We are rated on our aptitude as a teacher, principal, counselor, school and basic human being by The Tests. If we have a life outside The Tests by raising a family or engaging in any type of entertainment, hobbies, or interests it must be done in secret so that it appears The Tests are our sole focus and what we exist for. I believe we are secretly monitored every moment of our lives according to our commitment to The Tests, but I might just be getting a bit paranoid. I could swear I've seen miniature cameras throughout my house and heard clicking noises on my phone, though. Just in case, we've changed our boys' names to Data and Percentile and we speak in code. Saying Percentile, Data, and No Child Left Behind in the same sentence means, "Which one of you boys stopped up the toilet and stunk up the bathroom?"

I've seen adults disappear forever after getting their test results and I'm convinced they were taken out by The Test gurus, but maybe that's the paranoia talking. I've formed a group that has gone underground to live where The Tests can't find us. So far I have three members; me, myself, and I. We all feel extremely safe.

Therefore, every moment in school is spent on how to improve our test scores. We begin each school day with e-mail messages announcing in huge colored font how many days until we test. It is as big a countdown as when the astronauts launch into space. What is completely ridiculous is that in preparation for The Tests we test the kids all year as practice until they are completely comatose so that when the real tests occur in April they are so tested out they don't do so well on the tests that count.

Makes perfect sense.

Students' lives are not taken into consideration with The Tests. Students from preschool through high school are beaten, hungry, tired, cold, depressed, on medication, on street drugs, raped, drunk, hung over, homeless, helpless, withdrawing from nicotine, strung out, pregnant, addicted, caffeinated, abused and tired. (And don't even get me started on the public schools!). Yet, they all must perform at high levels on The Tests so that we, who all have bachelor's degrees, master's degrees, and more, must prove our worthiness by our test scores to teach our youth. The same youth that our politicians deem worthy of huge budget cuts at an alarming rate every year.

Makes perfect sense (if you are a moron).

This is all so that our legislators (see above about morons) who know less than nothing about schools, teaching, curriculum, brain research, learning theory, lesson planning, motivating students, and plain common sense can prove to all constituents and each other that we are showing up to work every day and doing our jobs and being the professionals that we went to college and earned diplomas to be.

If a dentist repeatedly tells her patients to brush and floss and stay away from sugary foods but the patients don't and keep coming back with cavities, does the dentist lose her job?

No.

If a doctor tells her overweight patients to exercise and eat low fat foods and less calories but the patients don't and have heart attacks, does the doctor lose her job?

No.

If the teacher tells her students to get their heads off the desks, pay attention, do their assignments, study for tests, stay away from drugs and alcohol and promiscuous behavior, and the students get drunk, pregnant, skip school, sleep through class, and fail tests and classes, does the teacher lose her job?

Yes.

Does the principal lose her job?

Yes.

Makes perfect sense. (Again.......morons).

Being the dedicated professional that I am, I made sure I reported to work after my surgery on the Monday of The Tests to ensure our students performed at their very best and therefore our planet could continue to spin on its axis and life could continue as we knew it. Then I proceeded to sleep in my car, causing panic in my co-workers who couldn't find me. Like I said, I believe I deserve major points for even being there.

The day came to receive the surgery results. Again, I dressed to kill. Again, nobody noticed. I had to put on a paper gown big enough for a toddler. After waiting at least three years, or so I thought, six people in lab coats filed into the examining room, taking up all breathable space. My surgeon was all smiles. I was not. I was too nervous. My doctor congratulated me on the results. My tumor was smaller than what they thought. It was 1.5 centimeters instead of two centimeters. The lymph nodes were clean (praise God from whom all blessings flow!). The margins of the tumor were clean. The second site was nine millimeters and was not cancer. The cancer was stage one cancer. I could breathe again.

My surgeon spent hours with me explaining all, answering all, and telling me all. That's when I lost it all. I didn't want chemotherapy. I didn't know enough about radiation to know if I wanted that, but I knew I didn't want to put poisonous chemotherapy drugs in my system. I said I didn't care about hair loss or other side effects, but I was completely terrified about poisoning my system. I begged him to remove my flat droopy breasts because they were a nuisance banging against my knees when I walked anyway, and I really didn't mind picking out perky 18-year-old looking ones as replacements. He explained that I needed the chemotherapy in case even one cancer cell got loose and was floating around my body looking for somewhere to land and multiply. I was crying. The doctor's assistant was rubbing my back. My hubby was flattened against the wall to keep from sliding down it. The doctor was very patient and kind. He said the treatments would be difficult, but they would be over in four months and then I could resume normal living. He said he and I would grow old together, and that was when I knew it.

The guy had a major crush on me.

I could understand why. I mean anyone would be captivated by my sweat stains through the paper gown, the clumps of mucous pouring down my face as I sobbed, and by how far I could spew snot. I was a vixen, a diva; a mess.

I went back to work the next day.

I made the appointment with the dreaded oncologist.

He was very serious, very efficient, and very brilliant. While he was explaining imperative information to Curtis and me I spent my time creating a personal goal. I must make him laugh. Didn't he read in my chart about my wit? Didn't he see how much fun I can be? Couldn't he realize that I was a laugh a minute? Apparently not, because he continued droning on in huge multi-syllable words in a medical language completely foreign to me. If I could make him laugh this nightmare would not be so horrific. Things would not be so huge; so scary. If he laughed we would be speaking my love language instead of his. My staggered thoughts consisted of the mantra: "Must. Make. Him. Laugh. (Or even chuckle).

He told us the two types of chemotherapy I would be getting, the dosage, effects, blah, blah, blah. I kiddingly asked him if I could get brain damage from chemotherapy. He didn't laugh like I thought he would. He said there was a phenomenon called Chemo Brain which affects people's memory and sometimes people recover from it and sometimes they don't. He said there was no explanation for it, no cure, and no medical definition for it.

Geez, that didn't turn out like I had planned.

I tried another tactic.

I asked him if I should continue with hormonal birth control. He asked me if I was finished having babies. I immediately replied,

"I'm not, my husband is, and my boyfriend is unsure". Nobody laughed, especially my husband. I think it was then I saw my brilliant oncologist notate in his file in big letters "Nit Wit". See, I knew he would notice my wit.

The three of us; me, my husband, and my amazing sense of humor departed.

I went back to work the next day.

I made the appointment for my first chemotherapy.

I asked the receptionist how long I would be there, thinking perhaps it took 15 minutes or so and since I was planning my day I thought I might be able to squeeze in a bit of time for some toxic chemotherapy. She told me five hours. I said I wasn't moving in, just getting chemotherapy. She said something unintelligible under her breath that I am sure rhymed with loser and scheduled me for the day reserved for difficult patients.

I was still completely frazzled about the chemotherapy. I absolutely did not want to go this route. Curtis, being the completely supportive spouse, continually berated and threatened me if I didn't go through with it. He assured me that he would help me through it. My Sunday School class prayed fervently for me.

One Sunday morning it was announced for women to surround me and touch me while the class prayed for me. It was so comforting to have those who loved me hold me physically as well as hold me up in prayer this way. After class a woman named Denise said to me that all morning she was being prompted by the Lord to touch me. She said He impressed on her to put her hand on me. She explained she didn't know what to do because it would be just plain weird to come up to me and say, "I'm supposed to touch you". I didn't say it, but I knew it would have been even weirder when I punched her lights out for doing it.

She didn't know what to do, but when the announcement was made to touch me and pray she knew that was what the Lord was prompting. What a blessing! If you don't know the Lord and haven't experienced Him and How He works, this could seem strange to you. I knew I was being blessed by God, that He was in control, and He was prompting others to pray. I was encouraged.

After class it was announced that anyone who wanted could meet in a circle to pray for me. The prayers that day were the most beautiful prayers I had ever heard. They were perfect prayers targeting specific needs I had. One person prayed for angels to surround me and protect me. Another prayed regarding my first chemotherapy treatment coming up. Someone prayed specifically for Curtis and Alex and Benjamin. Someone else prayed for my healing. Another asked God to cause the chemotherapy drugs to seek out and destroy any unhealthy cells lurking in my body. Another person prayed regarding my fear of the chemotherapy. Another prayed regarding the effects of the drugs.

By the time I went home that morning I was walking on air and didn't have a care in the world.

Lesson: Prayer is powerful. Do not wait for an emergency to intimately know the One to whom you are praying.

Panic Attacks Do Not Help

During another Sunday School session Gailen was teaching a lesson about Hebrews 13 regarding feeling others' afflictions. He explained that neither he nor anyone else could take on my cancer for me, (rats!) but others could commit to something for the betterment of themselves or others for four months while I was going through treatments.

He was suggesting the class use my cancer for good.

He proposed that anyone who wanted could commit for the next four months to go through the trial with me. He started by stating he was going to commit to losing 15 pounds during the four months of my treatments and instead of eating at his normal pace (and what a pace this is) he would pray for me. Then he asked others to commit to something.

I went cold and broke out in a sweat. This was going to be just like Friday nights in seventh grade. I was immediately transported back to the local ice skating rink with the boys circling the ice, seeking out cute girls lined up on the sides to ask to skate (while holding hands!). I knew I wasn't going to be asked to skate. I knew nobody was going to commit to four months of sharing my misery.

I was wrong (about the last one at least).

People's hands went up. A list was made on the board. Mary committed to restoring her relationship with her daughter. Diane committed to memorizing scripture. Debbie committed to exercising daily. Cyndi committed to praying for my family on certain days. Jennifer committed to the other days. Kim committed to sending me an encouraging card every week. Paul said he would bring his babies to me to play with. Phil promised hugs. Julie said she would take the night shift and pray for me during the nights. By the time they were finished there were 18 commitments on the board. These friends were going to go through the trial with me.

I didn't deserve such love.

Curtis and I sat crying and holding on to each other.

I decided cancer was great!

The day of my first chemotherapy treatment arrived.

I decided cancer was absolutely not great.

I threw up the night before just thinking about chemotherapy. I couldn't stop shaking from fear. We all knew Hubby would be a mess if he attended so he was given a free Get Out Of Chemo pass from me.

Debbie picked me up. I hauled 12 books, a laptop computer, water bottles, a personalized blanket (sent from a fellow counselor who said the room might be cold. All counselors are angels) and all of my emotional baggage into her van. I was leaving, never to return the same. I would come home toxic.

I secretly called the oncologist office before Debbie arrived to try to get out of my appointment. I told the receptionist I was coming down with a cold and I knew they wouldn't want to compromise a system that was already feeling compromised. I threw in a few coughs and sniffles for effect. She didn't buy it.

We somehow got to the doctor's office. Debbie parked the car. She reached for my hand and prayed for me. She got out of the car. I didn't. I couldn't. I opened my car door, which I thought was a step in the right direction. Apparently it wasn't because I was expected to get out and walk toward the building. I got out. I stood frozen in place. I was crying. My legs would absolutely not move! There was nothing on earth that was going to get my legs moving forward. They were completely rooted to the concrete.

Debbie came over to me, put her hand on my back and gently shoved me from behind to get me moving. Debbie is an enigma. She is all southern charm, blonde, tiny, sweet, and gentle. She lives on a farm. Think of Ellie May of the Beverly Hillbillies with a high I.Q. Scratch her surface and you've got an extremely strong-willed, steel-resolved tigress. That tigress was getting me into that building. I knew what I was up against.

She got me to the building. She got me in the doors. She got me to the desk where I frightened the receptionist with my hysterics. She got me to a seat. The receptionist started asking me really hard questions like what was my husband's cell phone number. I couldn't answer any of them. I lost all mental functioning.

We sat there for an hour. Debbie talked to me; I stared catatonic-like back. I finally opened my mouth to say I absolutely could not do this and therefore was leaving when the door opened and my name was called.

I was expected to walk to the nurse. I was expected to cover that long expanse of ground between him and me. It was the same path inmates take on death row to their execution. I was sure of it.

Another shove from behind and I was through the door. The nurse sat me down, took my blood pressure, pulse, and heart rate. Then he did the unforgiveable. He instructed me to step on the scale. I could tell he was actually serious. I started sizing him up to determine if I could take him down and make a run for it. As if I wasn't going through enough, now they wanted to humiliate me by weighing me!

Cancer was bad. Very very bad.

I put one foot on the scale and instructed in a very loud voice for all within a two mile radius to hear that nobody was to look and he was not to utter the numbers aloud. I checked Debbie, who I outweigh by about 100 pounds, to make sure her eyes were averted. All clear, I stepped on the thing. It was way wrong! It weighed me nine pounds more than my correct scale at home! The indignity! The humiliation! When I hotly commented this scientific fact to the nurse, he grunted and led me and all my trappings into the examining room. I sat on the examining table.

I burst into tears.

It was too hard, this chemotherapy thing. I wanted out of there.

The door opened. In walked Dr. Serious. He took one look at me and exclaimed in shock,

"My goodness! Are you alright?"

I wailed, "They just weighed me and your scale has me nine pounds more than my scale!"

He was speechless.

His adrenal system immediately went into overdrive and I saw the 'fight or flight' look in his eyes. He finally decided to stay and fight. He explained a lot to me, but I heard absolutely none of it. He said something about coming back in 24 hours for a shot and how often I would come for chemotherapy but nothing registered. My steel magnolia friend Debbie was listening for me.

Dr. Serious said I would do much better when I got into the chemotherapy room. What? This was not that room? No, I had to walk another death row mile to that room.

He lied.

When he took me into The Room I was not much better at all. I burst into tears again. When Debbie pushed me down into a chair, more tears.

I had never been in a chemotherapy room. It is a large room with leather reclining chairs all against the walls with reclining people all attached to I.V. poles. There were nurses flitting around hanging bags on the poles, giving shots, writing in charts, typing on computers, filling syringes, and checking notes. I learned later these were angels costumed as chemotherapy nurses.

The computers were down that day. (Of course they were). This meant there was much more activity when I walked in than normal. I was supposed to sit in chaos for five hours? After Debbie shoved me into a chair she produced a huge basket of items all wrapped in pink and put it in my lap. Where did that come from? She had it with her the entire time, but through my emotional distress and panic attacks I didn't even notice. Sheeesh! This counselor definitely needed intense therapy. I mumbled I would open the gifts when the chemo started. I hope I thanked her.

An older woman two recliners away from me started screaming. She was surrounded by her two adult daughters and a nurse who was giving her a shot in her

stomach. She was yelling how much it hurt and how nobody knew or cared how much it hurt. They were trying to quiet her. They were all making a huge commotion.

I stared, absolutely and completely horrified.

Then the nurse came toward me. I said in my very educated voice,

"You ain't coming nowhere near me!"

Yes she was, and she did.

She turned on the charm. She had a smile three miles long and she turned it toward me. She explained who she was (the devil as far as I was concerned) and she was going to give me a cocktail before the chemotherapy which was full of all kinds of fun things. I then made the fatal error. I asked her if I was going to lose weight through all of this, with the scale incident still fresh in my mind and all. She laughed and told me that they were pumping me full of steroids and the opposite would happen.

WHAT? I HAVE BREAST CANCER AND HAVE TO HAVE CHEMOTHERAPY AND I DO NOT EVEN GET ANY WEIGHT LOSS OUT OF IT BUT MIGHT (GASP) GAIN WEIGHT!!!????! ARE YOU ALL OUT OF YOUR MINDS?

I was so out of there!

Before I could escape my mother-in-law came through the door. I knew then there was no way out. She is another sickeningly sweet but fierce personality disorder. Why couldn't people be more like me; as obnoxious on the outside as on the inside? I don't waste time hiding anything in sweetness.

Miss Three-Mile-Smile came over and made nice to my guests. She had a bag with my cocktail and a needle for my port. Oh yes, my port. The one they put in during surgery to make chemotherapy more convenient and less painful. We found out that day that my port was in deep and turned at a funny angle and hurt like really really bad words when they tried and retried to access it. Over and over. Great. I was going to have to go through this pain every single time. My new prayer request; port access.

Smiles came over and hung the chemotherapy bag on my pole. I started opening gifts. I will always remember during the exact moment the drugs started entering my system I was opening presents from a friend. It was the most wonderfully awful thing! I didn't deserve any of it.

Lesson: When in doubt buy gifts

One day Curtis came home from work emotional and choked up. I asked him who died, hoping it wasn't me. He produced from his pocket a fat envelope given to him by his staff. It held hundreds of dollars' worth of gift certificates to local sit-down restaurants, coffee shops, and fast food restaurants. He was amazed by his co-workers' generosity and felt very humbled. I was wondering if the human race finally took pity on my family because they heard about my cooking skills, or if this gift was to keep my family fed while I was flat on my back on the couch. It didn't matter. It was a beautiful gesture that rescued me time and time again from my family standing in a semi-circle around the couch, staring down at me wondering when I was going to get up and cook something. I wondered if a woman thought up the gift certificate idea because it was so perfect. If not, the guy who thought of it will make a great wife!

Lesson: When in doubt, buy gift certificates.

God Did Not Create The Scale. Another Male Did.

The receptionist did not lie. I was there for five hours. Friends came and held my hands. Others brought more gifts. Gailen called from a field trip with his son in Washington D.C. and admonished me to keep myself together because others were watching me. When I left I felt like I had been there for a week. My mother-in-law was going to take me home. We were going to stop at the pharmacy to fill some anti-nausea prescriptions first. As we stood in the store waiting for my medicine and talking, it happened. I couldn't remember what I was talking about in mid sentence. I forgot what I was saying. I forgot words. I even forgot the subject. Chemo Brain. Oh! My! Gosh!

We went home and I relayed all of the horrible details of the day to Curtis. I kept forgetting words, thoughts, and people. He noticed right away. I was not the same woman who kissed him good-bye that morning. We had truly stepped in it now.

Dinners continued arriving at my door; casseroles, pasta, stews, soups, salads, desserts, vegetables, meats, potatoes, Italian, Mexican, and American concoctions. Meals I couldn't pronounce and more I couldn't even spell. I categorized it all in two words: Comfort Food. It was fabulous! We couldn't eat it all. We invited friends over nightly to help.

Every time the doorbell rang my boys would exclaim how great cancer was. It became like a sports cheer. The neighbors probably wondered why there was cheering every time they heard our doorbell. It was like Pavlov's dog. We would hear the doorbell and everyone would cheer, salivate, and slobber down their chins.

The boys' friends, the ones who are here so often we use them as tax write offs (don't tell Mr. I.R.S), also began exclaiming how great cancer was when they became the nightly recipients of those fantastic meals. I also would have exclaimed how great cancer was but I couldn't remember how anything was with my new forgetful personality. I decided I had to take their word for it.

Lesson: Make sure you have a big enough refrigerator. You never know when you will need it.

I continued going to work because I was such a mature adult. I felt very peculiar the day after my first chemotherapy treatment. My head hurt with strange spasms of sharp pain, I was dizzy, and I had constant diarrhea. The nurse said I wouldn't get diarrhea with the two types of drugs I was receiving. Someone forgot to mention that to my spastic colon.

I went to the oncologist the next day for my shot. It was explained that I would get the shot twenty-four hours after each treatment to build up my white blood cells because the chemotherapy drugs would absolutely ruin my good health. This medicine was designed to build up the white blood cells in my bone marrow.

I was awake the entire night before because of the steroids they pumped into me with my cocktail. I had never had steroids before. I decided I hated steroids. I noticed while getting ready to go to the doctor that my chest seemed a little pink. I checked into the office, all by myself this time, and waited for my name to be called. When I walked through the door the nurse told me to get on the scale. Again? I was just weighed yesterday. There was no negotiation. I got on. Then the nurse proceeded to scream out my weight for all of America to hear. I stared at her in complete shock. Who was she, Daughter of Satan? Why would she do such a cruel thing? How could anyone hate me that much? Dear God, would it never end?

The nurse from the previous day showed up. I mentioned I was a little pink. He informed me I was lit up like a Christmas tree and that it was from the steroids. He said I would look like I had bad sunburn for a day or two each time I had treatments. Nice. I was glowing but it wasn't like Moses after he met with God on Mt. Sinai. It was like falling asleep on the beach and burning to a complete crisp like a total idiot.

I got my shot. Satan's Daughter gave it to me in my stomach.

I went home to see what was being delivered for dinner.

I woke up the next day and couldn't move.

It was forty-eight hours after my chemotherapy treatment. This was to be my "bad" day. The day the full effects of the chemo drugs kicked in. The day of nausea. The day on the couch. The day from hell. I found out there would be many days of this, but they were not days, they were weeks and months.

The bone marrow shot must have been working because I was in so much bone pain I couldn't move. I felt every bone in my body and they were all screaming at me at the top of their lungs. I had to have help to move in any direction, but nobody was home. I stayed on the couch, not moving, eating, or drinking the entire day. I felt so horrible I didn't even notice I needed help. I stayed in one position, miserable and helpless and crying from the pain.

Later, I walked like a ninety-five year old woman hanging on whoever was unlucky enough to be near me. Actually, a ninety-five year old woman could have danced hip hop around me at that time. It was absolutely awful. I remembered the nurse told me that the effects of this shot could be intense bone pain for three or four days or mild bone pain for three weeks. My scenario was excruciating bone pain for ten days. How could my body hurt this bad? Dear God, they've made me into a cancer patient!

During this time I began asking Curtis for my own personal Get Out Of Chemo pass. I couldn't fathom going back for more. I was nauseous, I had sores in my mouth, I couldn't remember my name, I couldn't taste, I couldn't sleep, my bones still hurt, my nose and mouth were bleeding, and I was just plain sick. He said no. I begged him. He said no. I pleaded. He said no. I made bribes. No. I threatened. No. I yelled. No. I cried. No. I even considered offering sexual favors but I was afraid he would take me up on them. I lost the fight and went back for more.

During this second visit I was back on the scale, but this time I was ready. Hands on hips, I loudly tattled on the previous week's nurse who blabbed my weight for all to hear. The nurse called her a rookie and then silently wrote down my numbers. That settled, I went into the exam room. I was better this time. When the doctor entered he was not met with a hysterical or out of control woman. He was met with me, complaining that his scale was still broken.

He asked how I was. I told him. He prescribed stronger anti-nausea meds and stronger meds for the bone pain. He asked about my hair. I said I thought it was a cute cut on me and was thinking of a new style with highlights and long bangs but I couldn't decide on what colors to use for the highlights and did he have an opinion for me? I'm sure he had an opinion, all right. He rolled his eyes and said he was asking if any of my hair was falling out. I flippantly said it was all there and accounted for. He said if it was going to fall out it normally happens on day 21 of the treatments. He said I had a 75% chance of losing my hair. I wouldn't lose my eyebrows, he explained, so all was not lost. I was so comforted.

Lesson: Don't ever take your eyebrows for granted.

I was led into the chemotherapy room and "poisoned up". My sisters came. My mother-in-law came. Debbie was with me. This time she brought another huge basket filled with cards, stories, and anecdotes written from friends in our Sunday School class. This time, as the chemotherapy drugs entered my system, I was reading words of encouragement from friends. Again, I was so undeserving. I laughed, I cried, I was warm and fuzzy all over.

The next morning I was getting ready for work. I pumped hair product into my hand and proceeded to run it through my hair. My hands came away with more than they bargained for; clumps of hair. The more I ran my fingers through my hair, the more my fingers were covered in it. It was day 15 and I was losing my hair. Oh. My. Gosh.

I have short sassy hair. It is dark and extremely straight. Once when I was getting my hair cut from someone new to my head she remarked that she had never seen hair as straight as mine and my hair even lacked the ability to bend. This is why I have an on-going love affair with hair products. Stylists love me. They start counting the profits from what I'll buy before I'm even through the salon doors. As long as hair products exist there will never really be a recession in my world.

Although I could never make my hair curl or bend, I could at least give it the appearance of texture and thickness. I had a shampoo for fullness, an after-shampoo product for thickness, a thickening lotion for pre-drying, a paste for post drying, and a spray to wrap it all together. I've had my hair spiked, bobbed, angled, razored, teased, tossed, and textured. Praise the Good Lord for hair products. I secretly wonder if God could be a girl because nobody but a female could understand this love affair with hair products and allow them to be created in the first place.

On the morning my hair products failed me I decided I was not going to let my hair go thinner each day. It was all going to have to go at the same time. That evening I packed my two boys in the van and drove to my hairdresser. The manager ushered us to a remote corner. I asked her to put hair clippers in each boy's hand. I then told them to "have at it and have fun". They were tentative at first but quickly got into the spirit of the moment by deciding to give my head stripes. They mowed paths of stripes on my skull. Then they went for a Mohawk. They gelled the top of my hair to stand straight up. Then they went in for the kill and shaved it all off. I made sure I was laughing and whooping it up with them for their emotional health. It worked. They were fine. I was not. The manager took lots of pictures with my camera of this momentous event. I made sure I was laughing in each one.

Thankfully, the salon was in a mall. I exited the shop and immediately went into the nearest store and bought the first three shirts I saw. I figured losing one's hair justifies new outfits. I had never bought things so fast. I didn't even stop to try them on to see if they made me look fat. We then went out to dinner. Curtis had a meeting, so he missed all the fun. And it was fun. We made bald jokes all through dinner. I wore a pre-bought hat and we laughed about taking it off and scaring the other patrons.

I was in bed when Curtis came home that night. He knew about our evening so he came in our bedroom and asked to see my head. I had a sleeping hat on because my head was cold. I took the hat off and Curtis exclaimed how cute and adorable I was. What a prince! (A liar, but still a prince).

Lesson: When it is a terrible situation that involves hair it is okay to lie.

I had to go to work the next day. How was I going to do that? Everyone knows how cruel kids can be. How was I going to show up looking this way? Oh Dear God, how to do this? School would be out in two weeks. Couldn't I just use my sick days and stay home the rest of this time? Professional and mature Curtis explained to me that I may need my sick days another time and since I was going to be looking for a new job it may look bad to my new employer to not finish this school year. Rats. I absolutely hate grownups with a passion. I couldn't fathom why I married one.

It took some doing but I managed to get myself into the school building by praying, taking lots of really deep breaths, putting on a cute hat, and hurling myself through the front doors. My co-teachers did the preliminary work for me before I got there. They explained to their students what was going on and had mini lessons on rudeness verses kindness. I received many compliments on my hat that day from the students. I was so encouraged I even took the hat off when it became too hot and scratchy. I was told what a perfectly shaped head I had and it was the perfect shape for baldness. I was told how cute I was. I decided to believe every single word.

Lesson: When it is a terrible situation that involves hair it is okay to lie.

During these last two weeks of school I left my hats at home. If I was going to be bald I was not going to be ashamed of it. I purchased a button off the internet that read "Bald Chicks Rule" and I wore it every single day. It helped that Curtis was at home telling me how cute I was and telling me not to wear the hats. I think he liked having a bald wife. It was unique. Maybe he really did think I looked cute. He built me up to face the world each day. It was perfect.

I began interviewing for jobs. I was a counselor at a middle school the year before. I loved my job and thought I would be there for a long time. The superintendant job opened in my district and Curtis applied. He got the job. There is a state law that explains he could not be my boss. He was in, I was out. I had to look for a new job. Although I was absolutely thrilled for Curtis, I had to hit the pavement looking for a new counseling position. When Curtis applied for the job we assumed if he got it I would just go get another counseling job in another school. It turned out that was the year there were absolutely no counseling jobs in our area. I checked our state web site several times every day looking for an opening and none appeared. I couldn't believe it. I cried the entire summer over this. That is when I got mad at God for not getting my way. I was a mess. Others noticed.

I swore I would never teach again. I taught for sixteen years and I had worked hard to move beyond that. I went back to school for a master's degree in counseling, and I considered teaching moving backwards for me. Our boys were enrolled in a Christian school with tuition, and I had to find a job in order to keep them there. What was I going to do?

I began interviewing for principal and assistant principal jobs. I am a great interviewer. I look good on a resume so I was granted lots of interviews. I interviewed at one very prestigious school for the assistant principal position. They were very picky because they thought they were prestigious enough to be. I was one of 21 applicants. The interview lasted two hours and was with a committee of ten people. There were so many people around the tables I had to shout my answers to their questions so all would hear my brilliant replies. I wowed them. After their seemingly 200 questions I asked the fatal question. I asked for a specific explanation of what they were looking for in an assistant principal since all schools use this position differently. The principal responded they were looking for someone to be assistant principal, athletic director, nurse, truant officer, and instructional leader. I asked them if God had applied yet.

If I wanted to be a nurse I would have gone into nursing. I knew as acting nurse I would tell the kids,

"Take the red pill, no wait …take the blue one. Oh, what the heck take them both".

I know my limitations. As far as the athletic director position went I knew I was in trouble when Benjamin wanted a new soccer ball one year and while strolling though a sports store I excitedly pointed out to him that I found the soccer balls. Benjamin proceeded to inform me that those were not soccer balls, but basketballs. Athletic director? I think not. I informed the committee as such.

I was pleased the next day when I received the call saying they were hiring some other schmuck to wear all of those hats but be paid for only one. I was told I came in second. My ego considered that really good.

My husband used to be a school principal. He reminded me that it took him three years of interviewing before he was granted his first principal position. I knew that but I needed one NOW because I did not want to go back to teaching. Curtis reminded me that we do not always get what we want and that we are not in control, God is and He knows what is best for us. Sometimes there is such a fine line between love and hate in a marriage.

I continued interviewing. I continued coming in a close second. Something very weird was going on. I always got whatever job I interviewed for. This was new to me, and I did not like it one bit. I was sending out so many resumes I had to keep going to the store for more ink cartridges for my printer. I was spending a fortune on postage. I kept one eye on the calendar as I was begging God for a position. It was getting later and later in the summer. Jobs were getting filled. Jobs were going to stop being posted. Time was running out. Why wouldn't God open a door? Didn't He realize I deserved an administrative position? Didn't he get it that I absolutely did not want to teach again? I was too good for that! I would not go backwards in my career, I just would not! I was getting depressed. I was sliding so fast and far into a depressive state I think I broke something when I landed.

I spent the first half of the summer trusting God to do something wonderful. I spent the second half of the summer being furious with Him for not doing it. It was a fatal error on my part. It got so bad I only showered on interview days. Believe me, others noticed.

The boys were praying about the situation. Their friends were praying. Sometimes we all prayed together; me, the boys, their friends. Curtis was at work praying each morning. We all prayed together at night. It was not like the situation was not completely covered in prayer. God had it completely under control. Too bad I was completely out of control.

I sat the boys down and explained to them that if I did not have a job by August 15th they would need to leave their Christian school where their dad graduated and which their uncle started and go to public school. How were they with that? They responded they thought that was great. Alex informed me the reason God had not given me a job yet was because he and Benjamin knew that God wanted them to go to public school and God was holding out until that happened.

What?

I was floored. Not only were they completely okay with changing schools, but they had the situation completely explained and wrapped up in a nice package with a pretty bow on top. Well, that was certainly a new twist on things. I asked the boys if they would want to go to the local public school or to school with their dad. They said they wanted to go to school with Dad. Wow!

My boys are much wiser than me. It turned out God waited to give me a job until my boys were in public school. Immediately after they started school I was given a job teaching special education in a different school district. I was still mad at God. My backside was smarting from that fast and furious slide down the career ladder and landing at what I considered the bottom. I forced myself to eat huge slices of humble pie and go to work. I was humiliated to be a teacher again and even more humiliated to be teaching special education. There is absolutely nothing in the world wrong with being a special education teacher. Some of the most talented teachers I know are special education teachers. I knew I was not talented in that area and shouldn't be there. I could never be as great or even as good as those teachers that I admired. Could it get any worse?

Lesson: Do not ask if it can get worse because it can and it will.

I cried every day on the way to school and every day on the way home. I cried every day in the bathroom at school. I cried into my pillow every night. I cried just thinking about this job. I hated this job. I stopped crying after about four months, but I was still angry at God. How could He allow me to end up here?

There was one concession to this mess. The people I worked with were fantastic. They were wonderfully caring individuals who were great at their jobs. My co-workers made the days bearable. They were a lot of fun to be with. They also liked to party, which was right up my alley. I tried to make the best of it. Perhaps I was resigning myself to the situation. We got a new science teacher in October who ended up being my new buddy. We had a lot of fun, which to me is really the only reason to go to work; to continue the social life one has at home. I somehow made it through one day at a time. By April I had new friends, a horrible job, and cancer.

Now I was showing up to this awful job bald.

I was also starting to interview again because if it was okay with God I did not want to be there another year. I was hired last so when the school was going to have to cut positions I knew I was going to be the first to go. I needed out of there. I went bald to an interview for a principal job. I knew I did not want this particular job. It was at an alternative school for very difficult students (subtle for scary, dangerous, and out-of-control youth). I could hear my dad's voice in my head yelling at me that it would be very poor character to pull my name as a potential candidate after the date was set for the interview, so I made myself go. I also thought I should try for every job opening in case one of them was the job God had for me. I knew better than to let any opportunity pass, even the ones I thought I didn't want.

I showed up completely bald. I was very sick that day. I was prostrate on the couch the entire day trying to get strong enough to get up and into the shower and out the door by 3:00. Again, I was interviewed by a committee. It is easy to wow one person in an interview, but when you are before a committee you know everyone is looking for something completely different. Each person is hearing your answers differently. Each person has his and her own agenda. It's a very hard way to get a job.

I am sure the committee members took one look at my bald head and wrote me off as too sick for the job. One woman on the committee later told my husband she was completely and totally impressed with my ability to come to the interview bald because she knew she could never do such a thing. I knew I could do it because Curtis was at home telling me how beautiful I was. I give the women on the committee credit for not whipping out their lipsticks and using my shiny head as a mirror to apply them during the interview. I think if the roles had been reversed I might have been the first one to do that.

Thankfully, I did not get the job. Later in the school year a student showed up with a gun at that school. Thank you, Lord, for keeping me from that situation. At another school where I was not granted the administrative position a parent showed up wielding a knife and making threats. Thank you, Lord, for keeping me from that. Another school that I interviewed for had a horrible accident that resulted in major law suits, stress, and negative publicity. Thank you, Father, for your answer of no. There are blessings when God says no. I have learned that.

Lesson: Thank God when His answer is no.

The same week I interviewed for the job I knew I did not want, I interviewed at a high school for a counseling position. Again, I was sick and on the couch all day, but this time I wore a hat to the committee interview. The committee was made up of all women; the principal, the assistant principal, the two counselors staying, the counselor leaving, and the guidance department secretary. They were a lot of fun. It didn't feel like an interview at all. It seemed like a group of ladies chatting over coffee. I liked them and they liked me. On the last day of school, in what I consider poetic justice, I was offered the counselor position at Grant County High School. I accepted. Now I could just have cancer. It didn't matter that a few weeks later one of the school districts I had previously interviewed with called asking me to consider being their assistant principal. I had this job from God and I was excited about it.

Lesson: God knows better than us what is best for us. Wait for His direction.

A T-Shirt For A Cause

I absolutely love summer. I love not working and all it enables me to do such as playing with my boys, shopping, going out with friends, lounging at the swim club, sleeping late, staying up late, reading books, exercising, writing, taking walks, and goofing off. I hated this summer. It was spent on my back on the couch, sick, hurting, lying on the floor if there was no couch, depressed because all foods tasted like cardboard, and going back and forth to treatments.

Although it was awful, there were many wonderful blessings. I was told by Curtis that I had to appear at church one particular Sunday. I was attending church each week, but I would miss the Sunday of my treatments because of being sick. Of course this particular Sunday was during my bad week. In my fog I heard Curtis insist I be there but I couldn't string two thoughts together to wonder why.

I walked into church. I saw Marvin, a fellow Sunday School class member, in a t-shirt. That was odd. He is always dressed in a suit and tie. I looked closer. Was that my name on his chest? Was I hallucinating? I hoped my name wasn't anywhere else on his body. I walked into our Sunday School class. I stood dumbfounded, mouth hanging open, gaping, and it wasn't because of the doughnuts this time. The entire class had on t-shirts that said 'Kindred Hearts for Mary Beth' with the breast cancer symbol and our class verse; Galatians 6:10. The men had on black t-shirts and the women wore pink. Was this real? Was that Gailen and Randy, our two Sunday School teachers in (gasp) t-shirts? In Sunday School? At church? Neither one ever wore anything but a suit and tie to class, especially to teach! I was so doped up the reality of what my friends had done for me didn't sink in until a week later when I was more coherent and I saw a picture of everyone wearing their shirts. It was then I broke down and cried for the beautiful and wonderful support God had provided me. I felt so very unworthy. There was no way I was going to be able to thank them properly. Sarah, the friend who orchestrated the event, in my opinion, achieved sainthood that day.

During my treatments the class liked to wear their t-shirts to class outings and parties. Some wore them out to doctor's visits or shopping. They were stopped many times by people asking what they meant. It was a great show of unity to ourselves as a class, to me as someone needing support, and to God, whom we were all relying on. I decided cancer was beautiful. I've since learned they are still wearing the t-shirts which are still initiating conversations with strangers.

Some of the wonderful meals made for me were made by men. I had no idea the men in our class were such great cooks. Brian, a divorced father of four grown children, made fabulous comfort food consisting of homemade stew, salad, bread, and dessert. He was definitely speaking my love language! I knew he wouldn't be single for long with those culinary skills. I was right and am currently looking for something that fits to wear to his wedding next month. Another day two other friends, Dave and Russ, came by with arms loaded with multiple bags containing at least eight of every item off of the local burger joint. I am sure they spent a fortune. Although I couldn't get off the couch to eat it, my boys were in paradise.

I kept the door to our house unlocked and friends came in, tiptoeing past me on the couch and depositing their labors of love in my refrigerator. Moms came with small children, whispering reproaches not to wake me up. Older women came and dished out beautiful creations for my family. Friends filled and refilled my refrigerator with gelatin and popsicles at all times. Many left gifts with their meals.

One evening a mother-daughter team showed up to give me a pedicure and body massage. They left me buffed, filed, massaged, and loaded with new slippers and lotions. They were like a comedy team of errors. They were fussing at each other for forgetting cords, splashing water, breaking things, and creating messes. They yelled at each other, reminding the other that this was supposed to be calming and relaxing for me. They were adorable and made me miss my mom so much. Their bickering was an amusement they weren't planning on providing. I loved every minute of it.

My college friends took me out to my favorite restaurant where the desserts are as big as my backside.

Hmmm... maybe one causes the other........ I arrived at the table and we all burst into tears. We hugged and cried and made an awful scene. On the table were gifts just for me. I unwrapped a necklace with *Faith* engraved on it, specialty teas, a tea saucer, a scarf, and a pink bin to hold everything. It was perfect. Dear Lord, will your blessings never end? I hope not!

My sisters wanted to take care of me but my Sunday School Class was doing such an excellent job there was not much for them to do. We talked on the phone a lot. They brought meals whenever I would let them. My sisters are excellent cooks. I should have let them bring many more meals than I did. They attended my chemotherapy sessions and went shopping with me afterwards. My mantra was, "Everyone gets to buy something new on Chemotherapy Day". My mom had been gone for nine years and I noticed some of my sisters turning to my mother-in-law for solace. If Polly, sister number four, could not reach me, she would always call Marilynn. I was happy to share her. Marilynn was happy to offer comfort. I knew they were supporting me through their phone calls and offers of help.

There was one hole in this family support. I have two brothers. Robert is a year older than me and Pete is five years younger. I am sandwiched between the two, and I take great pride in being the only girl out of six who has an older brother.

Everyone was calling and checking on me. Pete was not. It became glaringly obvious that he was not calling me. At all. I was hurt. I mentioned it to my sisters. I asked if anyone had talked to him. I mentioned he had not called and I wondered why. I shared that I was trying not to be hurt over it, but I was struggling with it. Polly reminded me how sensitive Pete is and said she thought he was having a hard time handling my diagnosis. I tentatively agreed but I was still hurt. I was taking his silence to mean he did not care about me. Did he know I started treatments? Did he know I was bald? Robert called me just about every night. Where was my younger brother?

I continued treatments. Each time I went to chemotherapy I had a gang accompanying me. My sisters and I have a lot of characteristics we inherited from our parents. From our dad we inherited our strong opinions, sense of justice, and desire to fix every wrong we experience. From our mom we inherited our intuitive natures, our sense of humors, and empathy. Do not ever say someone is in need or you will have the Ruschell gang on you immediately, whether you want it or not. While at chemotherapy we would all make friends with anyone sitting nearby. There are a lot of us, so together we can be overwhelming. Even singularly we can be overwhelming. We would walk into the chemotherapy room strangers and leave everyone's best friend with new phone numbers, e-mail addresses, and promises to call. This might seem great, but I feel guilty about our party atmosphere. There were many extremely sick cancer patients hooked up to those I.V's. Some of them were not going to make it through their illnesses. We may have been too friendly, too loud, too much for some of them. To this day I feel guilt, wondering if we bothered anyone too sick to handle us. The nurses didn't say anything about it, but one week I noticed a sign on the door stating only one person at a time was allowed in due to the other patients' well being. I wondered if the sign was new or if I had just not noticed it before. In paranoia I then wondered if the sign was put up just on days I was coming in. I'll never know, but I am sorry if we were too much.

Pete was still not calling me. Polly said she talked to his wife who shared that Pete was still not over mom's death nine years ago and was not able to handle me being sick. He was dealing with my diagnosis by retreating. Although I heard the words, I was still bothered by them. A cancer diagnosis does not afford the luxury of retreat. It demands support in any way one can give it. My head knew my brother loved me. My heart was telling me other things. I vacillated between anger, acceptance, understanding, hurt, sadness, rejection, and feeling unloved. I love him. I know he loves me. I have since decided that loving each other is the only thing that matters.

Lesson: Cancer demands support, whether you feel up to the task or not. Retreating is not an option. I repeat, retreating is not an option.

Hurry Up And Wait

I t was time for my third chemotherapy treatment. The week before each treatment I would snuggle up to Curtis, look him full in the face, show him my puppy-dog eyes and softly explain that I could not go back for more and please not make me. His answer was adamant every time. I had to go.

After my third treatment my white and red blood cells were, as the nurses scientifically explained, "in the toilet'. I needed a shot to build up my red blood cells this time. This was another shot of a different type in the stomach. I think I was getting used to these shots in the stomach. I think the nurses were getting used to it also because there was less shocked gasping and horrified exclamations whenever I lifted my shirt. In fact, no one had fainted or left the room in weeks. I took my shot and went home.

Curtis and I and some friends went out that night. We were at a restaurant and I was almost finished with my meal. I started itching. I started scratching. I mentioned I must have walked into a mosquito nest unaware and proceeded to eat, itch, and scratch. We left and drove to the swim club to pick up Alex and Benjamin. I was beginning to claw at myself, creating huge welts while gathering stares from the club patrons. I was starting to become frantic with the itching. We returned home and I handed a bottle of anti-itch gel to Benjamin and asked him to rub some on my back. I lifted the back of my shirt and scared Benjamin speechless. Every inch of skin was completely covered in welts. I started wondering if it really was mosquitoes. I'm really smart that way.

I started getting scared. The itching was getting worse. We were outside and I was impaling myself against the edges of our brick house to scrape my back for relief. I was drawing blood on my back, arms, and legs. I called the doctor. While waiting for the on-call doctor to return my call Curtis told me to get in the car; we were going to the emergency room. We rushed to the ER where I proceeded to wait for four hours in abject misery; clawing at myself. I was itching from the inside out. I was a total mess.

I was finally called back to the examining room. It was decided I had an allergic reaction (you think?) to the shot I was given earlier that day. I was given an I.V., steroids (oh gee more of those), and other medications to counteract the reaction and sent home. While we were gone the on-call doctor called me back and Benjamin went looking for me to give me the phone. Alex informed him that I had gone to the emergency room. I am such a good parent I didn't even tell my child I was going to the hospital. When you are bald, sick, and clawing at yourself, it's a really good idea to tell all your children where you are going. No awards for me this year.

The next morning I woke up and couldn't see. My eyes were swollen shut. My skin was bright red and puffy.

I no longer had welts, I was the welt. Curtis called his mom and the doctor. Marilynn came over and gave me my medicine, put me to bed, cleaned my house, and did my laundry. Marilynn is a retired nurse from a time I know nothing about. Her philosophy regarding medicine is if one is good, two is better, and heck, three is probably best. She knew I was in bad shape so she was giving me medicine very often and in large doses to try to combat the reaction. It was not working. She was watching me very closely and carefully. So was my dog, only she was watching me more closely because she was in bed with me guarding me every minute. She knew something was wrong with me and stayed by my side constantly. While lying in bed or on the couch she would sprawl beside me or even on me if she could get away with it. Every few hours she would look up at me, lick my face, scratch herself and plop back down. I decided she would make a great husband.

Marilynn took me to the oncologist when we realized I was not improving. The nurses took one look at me and completely freaked out. I was immediately hooked to an I.V. pole and pumped full of everything they had.

While taking care of me the head nurse explained the shot they had given me was a long-acting shot which meant the reaction was going to be long acting. She feared since it was a Friday I was going to need more medical attention and I would end up in the hospital. I sat in the recliner, hooked up to an I.V. and cried like a baby.

81

I think I scared the other patients. I know I scared the medical staff. There was definitely not going to be a party this day.

By that night I was in the E.R. again. I got to wait another four hours before being seen by a doctor. I was out of my head in misery. They finally hooked me up and pumped me full of whatever sounded good at the time. I begged to be knocked out. I was delirious. Curtis, Marilynn, and sister number two, Becky, were with me. The doctor said they could not make me unconscious because of the dangers associated with that but they could give me "mind-altering" drugs. I was in a frenzy clawing at myself, bleeding, and crying. Mind altering sounded just fine to me. They gave me the drugs. They wanted to admit me into the hospital, but there were no beds available. I am told I became ugly. I tried to get out of the room to get a bed available. I showed my father in me by demanding this injustice be made right. I yelled they should not ask me if I wanted a private room and then tell me I could not have one. I exclaimed I would just march up to the correct floor and get a room ready by myself. I was attached to the bed by my I.V. which was a permanent part of the bed. I tried taking the bed apart. I demanded Becky call Pete and tell him what was going on. I demanded she call my friends. It was 1:00 in the morning and I was browbeating everyone in my path.

I remember none of it. I just know I was not the most popular patient they had that night and nobody on the medical staff was going to be sending me a Christmas card. Curtis said I was ugly to his mother which horrified me to no end. I kept apologizing to her after the ordeal was over but she kept insisting I had nothing to apologize for. She would tell me I had a lot of my dad in me and I knew then I had plenty to apologize for.

I was finally admitted. Curtis, Becky, and Marilynnn beat a hasty retreat to go home and lick their wounds from my tongue lashing. The nursing staff had me all to themselves. Poor creatures. I let any person who was unfortunate to walk by my room know that I wanted a private room. I only have snips of clarity from those four days and one moment of coherence was when I heard a nurse say very sarcastically to me, "Yes, we all know you want a private room, everyone knows you want a private room." I didn't know until much later that I threatened the staff with my brother-in-law, who is an attorney, if I did not get my way. I shudder thinking about what I know I said and what I still do not know I said.

Lesson: Practice your apologies before they are needed so that you have them handy.

Of course the four days in the hospital were a blur. I had visitors that Curtis told me later I had long conversations with. Debbie came and brought me a root beer float. If you don't remember it do the calories still count?

A pilot friend came to visit me. He told Curtis later he could tell I was completely drugged out of my mind because my eyes were darting frantically back and forth while I was holding court at my bedside. He was taught in flight training this was a sign of major drug use. Yep, I was on major drugs. So much so that I told the nurse I was not on any medication and then later when she gave me a pill I told her I was taking that at home. She stared at me, horrified, and said I had told her I was not on any medications. Hello! Why would you take the word of someone you were giving mind-altering drugs to? I was completely out of my head but nobody knew it because I was having normal conversations. (That tells you a lot about my normal conversations). Each day I was asked if I wanted a sponge bath and each day without knowing it I said no. I cannot imagine how I looked and smelled to my visitors.

I woke up one Sunday morning to my friend Cindy by my hospital bed. My first thought was I died and I'm in hell and Cindy is here because she got a trashy tattoo and I'm in here because of my association with her. I asked her what she was doing there and why she was not in Sunday School. She informed me I called her hysterically crying that morning and I was her Sunday School that day. Oh.

Having five sisters, I would think I am last on the list of someone needing another sister, but that is exactly what Cindy is to me. She is a second grade teacher, a mother of three, wife of one, and the edgiest Christian I know. By edgy I mean I am constantly amazed (and mostly scared) at what comes out of the girl's mouth. She has a butterfly tattoo on her lower back, dyes her hair half blonde, half purple, and thinks she's all that. She's the kind of friend that I can tell her she looks like trash and she takes it as a compliment.

Upon diagnosis I called Cindy and promptly told her,

"I have breast cancer and you are going to get me through it".

A tall order for anyone, but Cindy took the charge and kept me stocked with popsicles, Jell-O, visits, phone calls, prayers, meals, and now a bedside vigil with her slathering some kind of potion on my arms as a form of her Sunday morning worship. Every human being needs a friend like Cindy. She's the one who compared my cancer to popping a zit and told me to get up and get over it and get on with life. On second thought, maybe every human doesn't need a friend like her; maybe only the bad people. After my treatments she told me to get my name off the prayer chain at church because I was done and there were plenty of other people who had real prayer needs and I was taking prayer away from them. What a friend!

As a fellow educator we have much in common. We agree completely that education today is completely whacked out. She has some really great second grade stories. My favorite was the year she had a second grade student share with her that he was trying to quit smoking. We are both up against a lot of the same moronic issues in our work. We are both expected to perform miracles each day from a society that sends us undernourished, undervalued, and underachieving children. Many times she makes me cringe, but most of the time she makes me laugh, so I have decided to keep her. The only problem is she is in love with herself and I am in love with myself, and when we are together we must share the limelight with each other. It somehow works though.

Insurance, Anyone?

The day of my last chemotherapy treatment came. I was scared because each dose had me feeling worse. The nurses told me this was because chemotherapy has an accumulating effect. The more I got, the stronger it was building up inside my body. I again begged Curtis to let me out of it. He again refused. Stubborn does not begin to describe him.

When the doctor came in I had my plan ready. I was going to tell him it just was not going to work out between us and I was breaking up with him. I was sorry, but I had to move on with my life. I was planning on using all the standard break-up lines like it's not you I just need my space, etc. I didn't get the chance to use any of my lines. My doctor casually informed me this was not my last day to visit. He said I had to come back every three months for a year, every four months the next year, every five months the following year, every six months the year after that and then once the fifth year. I stared at him, dumbfounded. I was speechless for the first time ever.

What was with my doctors? They were all madly in love with me and wanted to spend the rest of their lives with me. I carefully explained to him that he had to get a life and I couldn't be the focus of it and to let go. He carefully explained to me that all patients have to come back for five years and I was to report back in January.

Oh. I get it, he was in denial. If that was how he wanted to spin it that was fine with me. I knew it was just a coping tool he was using to get over me. I was used to it.

With all of the trips to the doctors, hospitals, cancer treatment facilities, and surgeries I was racking up quite a huge chunk of bills. Fortunately, I had medical insurance that paid most of it. Unfortunately, I also had a cancer insurance plan that I bought because Curtis informed me one day his tumors could take an ugly turn at any time and grow cancerous. I felt like such the mature adult buying a family cancer plan. I believed we were covered in case of a cancer emergency.

When I started filing claims with my cancer insurance I was met with letters of denial. Each time I called I was told I needed the B-142 form from the hospital, not the B-163 from. I called the hospital and was informed they had never heard of the B-142 form. I called the insurance company back. They told me they must have the diagnosis on doctor letterhead with codes for this and numbers for that. I told them I had already sent that in. They said it was not on the right form. I called the doctor's office and they said they had never heard of that form and the one they used for me was the one all insurance companies use and accept. I called the insurance company back. They said I was wrong and they could not file my claim without the exact forms.

I was not falling in love with this insurance company, and I think I explained my feelings for them during more than one phone conversation. I tersely told them that having cancer was enough to have to deal with without their company making life so much more difficult by demanding nonexistent forms, signatures on certain papers, etc. One claim was denied because they said the faxed form was too light to read. They didn't bother letting me know this so that I could send another one, they just sent me another denial letter. I could have wallpapered my living room with their letters of denial. Instead, I used them as toilet paper.

I decided right then I no longer liked insurance companies At ALL. I was turned off by all of them. I cancelled my membership. Curtis came home a few months later and said he bought a new cancer policy for himself and the boys and also bought an accident policy because of the boys' involvement in sports. I was left out in the cold because having had cancer meant no company would take me on. We usually decide these things together, but Curtis couldn't get a hold of me at the time and went ahead and signed on the dotted lines. I told him that was fine, but if it were up to me I wouldn't ever open another policy with an insurance company. In my opinion they were all frauds. Sister number four sells insurance, so don't tell her I said that.

Lesson: If possible, talk to someone who has filed a claim with the insurance company before signing.

Breakfast Of Champions

I didn't get to play with friends or my boys at the pool that summer, but I compensated in other ways. Chemotherapy had finally ended and I had radiation treatments scheduled every day for 30 days. Although my radiologist was extremely competent, he looked so young I was worried about the radiation stunting him, causing him to never get through puberty. I formed a pattern of taking the boys to football, going to radiation, and then meeting a friend or sister for breakfast before picking the boys up. There is a silver lining in every cloud and my silver lining was breakfast out every morning during these mornings of radiation. Somewhere in there I began to taste food again, so that was an extra bonus. I took full advantage of my new-found taste buds because meals were still being delivered nightly to our house. Many nights two and three meals would come and we would of course turn it into a party with my in-laws and friends. I thought Gailen was going to cry when I announced enough was enough and I was ready, after four months of not cooking, to take over our family dinners.

He's had my cooking. I don't blame him for crying.

It was some time before he broke the habit of stopping at my house every night after work expecting a beautiful meal. Poor guy. I'm not sure he has completely recovered from it.

If Cindy is the sister I never wanted, then Gailen is the brother I never wanted. He scares most people and animals, but when you get to know him he's not so frightening. He has a laugh that could wake the dead and uses it often. It doesn't matter that he is usually laughing at one of his own jokes. He bosses me around like he owns me, and I tell him what he can do with his bossiness. The adults he scares just need to learn how to tame him. Like a rabid animal, you must put lots of space between him and you. Then, without ever looking him in the eyes, slowly take food out of your pocket or purse and approach him cautiously, slowly, and steadily. Lay the food at his feet and retreat quickly, never turning your back on him. Once the food is accepted by him you can start a conversation in a very low and soft voice.

He is a control freak who married another control freak. We go on vacations with them yearly and still carry battle wounds by episodes of the two of them fighting for control the entire time. Car rides with them consist of the passenger telling the driver to change lanes, go faster, miss that light, take this short cut, get ahead of that car, slow down, watch that cop, get in this lane, take this road, turn here, speed up. Each ride with them ends in me opening my door and falling to the ground in praise that the ordeal had ended.

They have totally ruined the camping experience. A simple act of cooking popcorn over an open fire becomes a herculean battle between the two where life and death rests on who gets the popcorn right. I am totally off popcorn for life because of them. I wish they'd fight over dessert, maybe I could get turned off by sweets. I'm surprised we go anywhere near them. We get along because Curtis and I are such sweet, easy-going, passive people. Well, Curtis is at least. He gets along with them.

Gailen was losing weight like he promised in Sunday School. Every few weeks he would check everyone's progress with their promises to go through the trial with me. It meant a lot to me. I informed him that I did not like the new skinny Gailen. Besides, because he was no longer eating he was no fun and of no use to me since we had only our love of food in common. He was constantly reminding me I was living my belief out loud during my cancer and I had better not blow it. Yeah, he has a talent for lifting people up that way.

Lesson: Make sure you have friends who like to laugh. You are going to need them.

I was told that radiation could make me tired. I scoffed at that. I could handle tired over sick, bloated, nauseous, bald, and incredible bone pain. I could do tired.

They didn't tell me that tired meant lying on a hardwood floor because it was too much work to walk all the way over to the couch, or that tired meant lying on my husband's office floor for two hours until I had the energy to drive home.

Remember the slogan for a fire in your house: Stop, drop, and roll? The slogan for my radiation was

Stop and Drop. Literally. When the radiation fatigue hit, I dropped. I laid on so many different floors I began to appreciate life from the new angles. It added perspective. It scared people when they happened upon me on the floor, but that just added more fun to the entire fun-filled experience of having cancer.

Benjamin had a birthday in July. We had a big dinner with cake and presents. Before we put the candles on the cake I realized I couldn't function another minute. I sank to the hardwood floor and enjoyed the rest of his birthday from below. Curtis joined me and everyone in attendance acted like it was the most natural event in the world for Benjamin's parents to celebrate a birthday from the floor. (That tells you what low people we hang out with). After forty minutes I was ready to get up and resume festivities.

Lesson: Cancer affords one the opportunity to be weird. (People tell me the cancer is over and I can stop now, but the weirdness is officially a habit).

Work, A Four-Letter Word

My new counseling job at the high school started in late July. I could hardly keep my head up because of the toll of the radiation and I hadn't even started working yet. I didn't know how I was going to start a new job in this shape. The skin on my breast was coming off and I was bleeding and oozing through my bra and clothes. I was not even finished with treatments when I was scheduled to start this new job. Dear Lord, how was I going to do this? I had to be at my best since I was meeting new people, and everyone knows first impressions are the most important. How do I pull this off? I could not go in there sick, tired, and oozing.

I did what I've done my entire life. I faked it. I deserve an Academy Award for my performance. I went to radiation at 7:00 each morning and then went to work where the entire world was a stage. I met new co-workers, I laughed, I conversed, I went out to lunch, and I worked; in that order. Every few hours I went into my office, shut the door, and applied and reapplied medication and changed dripping bandages. I would look at my office floor with longing wanting to lie down, but managed to wait until I raced home each day to fall into bed. I was pushing myself very hard. Much harder than the doctors liked. Much harder than my sisters liked. Being the youngest of six girls means my sisters think they can tell me what is best for me and boss me around, even during healthy times. Some were expressing displeasure at my returning to work so soon. I felt like I didn't have a choice. I couldn't say to my new employer and co-workers,

"Hey, thanks for hiring me. Some day in the future I will do a really good job here, and oh, did I mention I'm not at my best right now so I need to start later and let everyone do my portion of the work until I get back on my feet, whenever that might happen to be?"

I had to make myself go to work. I absolutely hate being an adult.

The first day of school for the students was going to start very soon. I was left with a dilemma; to wear or not to wear a hat. These 1140 students didn't know me. They had never seen me before. How would they react to a completely bald new counselor? Would they make fun of me? I didn't think my carefully constructed armor could withstand teenagers making fun of me. Curtis said to go to work and just be myself (as if that has ever worked for me). I decided Curtis is much wiser than me, so I prayed, took many deep breaths, and went to school.....without a hat.

The kids were perfect. I stood in the hallways during class changes and joked with them. I clowned around and got to know them. They got to know me. Not one negative word was said about my baldness. They loved my "Bald Chicks Rule" button. They were the most polite students I had ever worked with. Many students confided to me later that they thought I had shaved my head on purpose. They thought it was cool and matched my personality (or lack of personality). God bless the students and staff at Grant County High School! I was right where I belonged. God put me in the perfect place for me. I immediately fell in love with everyone there.

Lesson: God knows what is best for us. Wait for it.

I loved this new job. I constantly need new challenges, and the fast-paced days met my need for learning new things and being pushed. I went everywhere bald, armed with my "Bald Chicks Rule" button. Each morning I put my bald on. This was an attitude I made sure was in place before walking out my door. I believed if I exuded confidence others would fall for it. It worked. I acted like I didn't care I was bald. I acted like it was the most natural thing in the world. I acted like I was as cute as Curtis was telling me each day. It wasn't my fault I was bald, so I just went with it. I would not have chosen baldness, but since nobody asked me my preference and my hair fell out, I was going to make the best of it.

I am glad I did. I showed my boys what inner strength is. I showed them how to laugh when life gets hard. I showed them how to rely on God always. My new mantra for the boys changed from *"It doesn't matter how you play the game, what matters is how your hair looks while you're playing"* to *"what matters is how your hair is going to look during the game when it grows back in"*.

My hair started growing back in November. It started out as soft and fuzzy as a new-born baby which, by the way, looks great on babies but not so much on an adult. I had lost every hair on my body. I had not shaved my legs or shampooed my scalp in four months. Suddenly there was hair on my legs. I lost the peach fuzz on my head and real hair started coming in. My eyelashes started growing. My eyebrows, which I had been assured by my oncologist would not fall out but did except for maybe three hairs on each brow, began to thicken.

The only problem was it wasn't my hair growing back on my head. It was someone else's. It was in tight curls. Me, the owner of the hair that a professional declared 'lacked the ability to bend' was growing tight ringlets! God surely has a great sense of humor. I get lots of compliments on my short curly hair, but I cannot figure out if they are sincere compliments or if everyone is just so glad I have any kind of hair they think anything looks good.

It doesn't matter.

I have hair and it does not even need product! I consider my 'do' short, sassy, and low maintenance. Thank you, God! I was shopping the other day and a sales girl exclaimed loudly how much she loved my hair. She said it was cute! I decided to believe her.

Lesson: Give God thanks for everything. Always! Really!

Life Coach

I am glad God allowed me to have cancer. Although I never would have chosen cancer for myself, ever, I was afforded the opportunity to walk more deeply with my Savior because of it. I didn't have to search for God or hope He would rescue me from the terribleness of it all. He walked very closely with me throughout it and even carried me when I needed it. He filled my cup to overflowing with the blessings of His people through meals, gifts, letters, prayers, gestures, cards, phone calls, visits, cleaning, washing, massages, grocery shopping, etc... Each act from a friend was a form of worship for them and a blessing from God to me. It was perfect.

God is not a God who is to be called on only when life gets rough. God is to be enjoyed when life is good, too. Daily walking with our savior teaches us who He is, how He works, and what He thinks so that when times get severe we already know Him and can recognize Him working. It is not guessing; it is an actual knowing.

I met God when I was 25 years old. I always wanted to know about Jesus, but I had not met anyone who told me about him until I was in college. I was in a friend's dorm room and two new friends started casually talking about Jesus' return to earth. I stopped them and asked what in the world they were talking about. They explained that Jesus was going to return to earth at His Father's command and take His believers home. I questioned how they could possibly know this. They said it was in the Bible. I said,

"You mean we're really supposed to read that thing? I thought it was just some book full of stories". (I didn't tell them I secretly used to look at our big colorful family Bible while growing up because it was full of half-naked pictures). They informed me that the Bible was God's word written to us to know Him.

That gave me a lot to contemplate.

While in my car one day I was listening to a show on the radio explaining about God. The speaker was talking about eternity, knowing God, and Jesus' death. He explained that the reason Jesus died was because God is a completely Holy God and cannot tolerate sin. He absolutely cannot be anywhere sin is. Since we are all sinful we are cut off from ever being with God, now and forever. God then gave the best He had for us; His Son Jesus. Jesus was born so that He could die the death our sin would (and should) have caused us. He died our death for us; for me. Jesus bridged the gap between God and us so that when God looks at us He does not see sin, but sees His Son.

The speaker said in order for God to see Jesus when He looked at us was to pray and ask for salvation. He prayed a prayer and asked any listeners who wanted to repeat the words after him. He prayed,

"Lord, I realize I am a sinner who is cut off from you. I am sorry for being a sinner. I want to be saved. I want to be a part of your family for eternity. I realize being a good person will not allow me to get into heaven because I am sinful and you are Holy. Being good is not enough. Jesus is enough. I accept Jesus' sacrifice on the cross on my behalf. Save me, Lord. I am yours".

I repeated the words. I believed the words. I was saved. I was a Christian. My life would never be the same. I now had an advocate, Jesus, who would take my prayers to God. I now knew the One who had a plan for my life; who had my best interests at heart. I had a reserved place in heaven.

I spent the following 20 years learning about the One who saved me by studying the Bible, talking with my Savior, and seeing Him work. When I was diagnosed with cancer Curtis told me God was not the least bit surprised by it so I should just put on my seat belt and go along for the ride. That is exactly what I did. And what a ride it was. I can say the ride was great because God was my personal driver behind the wheel and orchestrating the trip. He has many more trips planned for me and as long as I keep allowing Him to be the chauffeur, I will be perfectly fine.

If I had not known God when I was diagnosed with cancer this trip would have devastated me and my family. We would have been completely lost, tossed around in a wreck that was just too big to get through. The carnage of my fear, disappointment, and worry would have paralyzed me. For all of my immature, loud, obnoxious, and impulsive ways I made one decision in my life that was right, honest, sincere, and true. I gave myself to my Creator. Then I learned who He is by joining a church that taught His word. I learned how to converse with Him through prayer. Then I put my seat belt on and let Him take me where He wanted.

He took me to Curtis, my perfect and beautiful gift, then to Alex and Benjamin; individuals who are a constant reminder of God's greatest blessings, to new jobs, new careers, new friends. He took me through a miscarriage and the death of my mom and then dad. He gave me the most wonderful in-laws that He ever created. He drove me through losing my job, and He stayed with me during the very bumpy and turbulent ride while trying to find a new one. Although I belligerently stomped off for a while when I didn't get my way, He stayed beside me leading me back. He waited for the perfect timing for a new job that He knew I would love.

Although the future rides are uncertain, I am certain of my driver. I will keep my eyes on Him and not on the road. If the "One who sticks closer than a brother" has cancer in store for me in my future, then He will guide me through it again.

A few months ago Curtis, Benjamin, Alex, and I were driving home from a weekend at a friend's lake house. The car was quiet. It was late. We were all subdued from a weekend in the sun and water. It was peaceful; the perfect opportunity to converse without fear of I-pods, cell phones, MP3 players, and other electronics taking center stage. I quietly asked the boys to tell me what they learned from our experience with breast cancer. I asked them to share who they saw me leaning on and what insights they had. I wanted to know if they learned positive life lessons from the ordeal or if I blew it and they were completely scarred for life (and still fixating on breasts).

Alex said he saw me leaning on God and Curtis. He said he saw the many ways friends had helped us and that he would do the same for others. He said he loved all of the meals and he noticed the many different ways people showed their support. He assured me he would help others this same way throughout his life.

Benjamin said he learned from me to praise God in every situation; the good, the bad…always. He said he would use this lesson throughout his life.

Curtis said I lived what I believed. He said I did a good job. He said he was proud of me.

My job was done.

Lesson: Glorify God in every situation. Praise Him always, especially through the storms, even when it doesn't make sense.

A Call To Action

Life can change very quickly. One minute I can weigh a perfectly respectable college-coed weight, and what seems like the next moment the scale and I are mortal enemies. One minute I am be-bopping and zig- zagging through life and the next second I have cancer.

My friend Gary came to my side during my first dose of chemotherapy. He sat on a hard uncomfortable stool and held my hand for many hours. He let me squeeze his hand as hard as humanly possible each time they tried to access my port. He lied and kept telling me I was doing a good job and I could make it through this. He was a professional at what I was only attempting. He had been on chemotherapy for many years and was battling stage four pancreatic cancer. Gary finished fighting, and a year after he walked me through my trauma, I was sitting at his funeral.

My friend Ric, who is a gifted artist, graciously offered to design the cover of this book. Ric was diagnosed with throat cancer earlier in the year. He finished his fight and is now painting with Jesus, using colors and textures he had no idea even existed. He is at the Potter's wheel, receiving instruction from a Majestic Potter.

Six months after I ended my treatments, Paul, the friend who offered bringing his babies to me to cheer me up (but I am glad didn't because I was too sick), was told he had prostate cancer.

After the holidays, my brother-in-law, married to sister number two, rang in the new year with prostate cancer.

I am agonizing over two wonderful women at church who have been told they have two and three months left to live because of liver and breast cancer.

The woman we sold our house to now has breast cancer.

My doctor friend from church who called me the day I received my diagnosis is now facing his wife's diagnosis of adrenal cancer.

What do we do?

We pray. And then we get to work.

Cancer is a call to action. It is a call to arms for those of us who are cancer free (at the moment). Once a diagnosis is official we are to snap to attention and form supportive battle plans that include giving until it hurts. We are called to getting sweaty and dirty in our single-mindedness to show support.

Every battle plan will look different. We are limited only by our own lack of ideas. Some battle plans include scheduled meals, gift certificates, rides to and from treatments, taking kids to school and practices, grocery shopping, picking up medicines, massages, and gifts of books, magazines, and pajamas. Others include church-wide garage sales to raise money, gasoline gift cards for a year, house-cleaning services, laundry services, pedicures, facials, manicures, lawn mowing, house repairs, jewelry fundraising parties, and babysitting.

Like my Sunday School class, the battle cry could include personal commitments to walk through the valley with an individual during the length of their treatments. It could include writing a book and giving the proceeds to people in need. It could involve sitting and listening to someone's fears.

Each battle plan is an opportunity to partner with God while walking someone through the cancer experience. Reaching out a hand to another offers the opportunity to show Jesus' nail-scarred hands to others.

Our God is an active and working God. He calls us to live our beliefs out loud. What do we believe in? Do we believe in the television? Let's turn it off and make a meal for someone. Do we believe in the computer? Let's unplug it and sit with a friend during chemotherapy. Do we believe in video games? Let's put them down and take someone their groceries. Do we believe in our own daily activities that keep us running at full speed? Let's miss one game or practice and make an encouraging visit to someone.

What if you are next? In the game of Tag you are touched and told, "Tag, you're it". What if cancer tags you and says, "You're it"? Do you personally and intimately know the One in control of your diagnosis? Do you follow the One who knows the number of hairs on your head and the exact number that will grow back after you are bald? Do you know how He works, what He believes in, what makes Him sad, angry, glad? Do you know His sense of humor? Do you know why His son has scarred hands and feet?

If so, cling to Him, thank Him for your cancer, put on your seat belt, and hang on to Him during the ride. The ride might include a time of sickness followed by good health. Your ride might include a prolonged illness. Your ride might include leaving this world to find yourself wrapped in His arms and no longer feeling any pain at all. Whatever your sickness brings, thank Him for it.

If you don't know your Redeemer (Psalm 19:14), Deliverer (Psalm 144:2), Savior (Isaiah 45:15), Lord Of All The Earth (Micah 23:8), The Life (John 11:25), Bright Morning Star (Revelations 22:16), I Am (Exodus 3:14), Tower of Strength (Psalm 61:3), Holy One (Acts 3:16), Chief Cornerstone (Mark 12:10), Righteous One (Acts 3:14), Bread of Life (John 6:35), Potter (Isaiah 64:18), Strength (Psalm 46:1), Refuge (Psalm 46:1), Holy One, (Habakkuk 1:12), Wonderful Counselor (Isaiah 9:16), King (Isaiah 6:5), Shepherd (Genesis 49:24), Rock (Habakkuk 1:2), The Beginning And The End (Revelations 22:13) (I could go on and on) don't wait for cancer to 'Tag' you to know Him. Pray right now.....you will find Him waiting for you and wanting to show you who He is and what life can be like with Him walking beside you.

I woke up one day and my hair was straight again. I love His sense of humor!

LaVergne, TN USA
05 February 2010
172244LV00002B/2/P